TEACHING YOUNG DANCERS

MUSCULAR CO-ORDINATION IN CLASSICAL BALLET

TEACHING YOUNG DANCERS

MUSCULAR CO-ORDINATION
IN CLASSICAL BALLET

JOAN LAWSON

WITH 140 PHOTOGRAPHS
AND 7 DIAGRAMS

THEATRE ARTS BOOKS
NEW YORK

FIRST PUBLISHED 1975

BY THEATRE ARTS BOOKS

153 WAVERLY PLACE/NEW YORK 10014

SECOND PRINTING 1979

© 1975 JOAN LAWSON

ISBN 0-87830-144-5

Library of Congress Catalog Card No. 75-15369

MANUFACTURED IN GREAT BRITAIN

CONTENTS

LIST OF DIAGRAMS

specially drawn by Gary M. James

LIST OF PHOTOGRAPHS

specially taken by Arthur Carter and Anthony Lawson

ACKNOWLEDGEMENTS

Many friends have given generously of their time and knowledge to help me write this book and to them I can only offer my deepest gratitude and by naming all, wish to place on record their interest and sympathy. This idea of working on the co-ordination and chain reactions of a dancer's muscles was originally suggested by the late Ivor Robertson F.R.C.S., whose exposition and understanding of would-be dancers' problems at his regular orthopedic examinations at the Royal Ballet School opened my eyes to the corrections and adjustments which it is possible to make in a child's physique. Sadly he did not live to comment on my work as he had promised. Instead my dear friend Stuart Steele F.R.C.S., M.R.C.O.G. of Middlesex Hospital has undertaken that task and I cannot thank him enough for his understanding and wise counsels both as a specialist and as a lover of ballet. Professor Tanner of the Institute of Child Health has also contributed to my knowledge, and J. Huwyler of Zurich, orthopedic surgeon and adviser to several leading European State Ballet Schools has furthered my studies in many different ways. I must also record my best thanks to Gary James of the University of Bristol for the infinite care he has taken to produce drawings which I feel confident will help readers to a better understanding of the problems discussed.

However, although the contribution made by all the above has made my work possible and so much easier, without the continued encouragement, co-operation and questioning of my colleagues at the Royal Ballet School, I should never have dared to attempt this book. I am always indebted to Dame Ninette de Valois and the late Ursula Moreton for giving me the opportunity to join the staff; to our principal Barbara Fewster for so many kindnesses and permission to use photographs of our students; to Pauline Wadsworth, Sara Neill, Pamela May, Julia Farron, Eileen Ward, Valerie Adams, director of student teacher training and Walter Trevor for helping to solve certain problems; to Arthur Carter of our academic staff for his patience and understanding when taking the photographs; to my friend Mary Clarke of *The Dancing Times* for innumerable kindnesses; to my niece and nephew Annabel and Jeremy Rees of the Arnolfini Gallery, Bristol for much valuable help; to my nephew Anthony Lawson and his Emma, and Mark Trevor for other photographs; and finally to Carina Fellstrom, Judith Gill, Susan Stanley and Stephen Beagley, whose valuable and willing co-operation and clear understanding of my purposes made our photographic sessions such happy and successful occasions.

Note for the second impression

I should like to place on record that Susan (now Siobhan) Stanley is dancing with the Sadler's Wells Royal Ballet, Stephen Beagley with the Royal Ballet and Judith Gill with the Hamburg Theatre of Opera and Ballet. All three are from time to time dancing solo roles.

Joan Lawson, August 1978

INTRODUCTION

CAN the gift of artistry in classical dance be undermined by poor physique or some structural anomaly? Can specific exercises be given so that the difficulty is worked on and overcome?

The answer to such questions is a qualified Yes. With great care and constant attention to detail, it is possible to overcome many of the difficulties arising from poor physique or some structural anomaly. But in some cases the natural bone structure of the pupil is such that no attempt at correction should be made.

Every movement in classical dance, as in life, sets up a chain reaction through the muscles of the body in greater or lesser degree. But whereas those in life are largely instinctive, if the performer possesses the normal faculties for movement, those in classical dance are of a more sophisticated nature. They are based on normal movement but have been refined by constant training. This is largely due to the need for turn-out which gives line to this form of dance, therefore the muscles have to be re-educated to work as correctly and as naturally as possible, bearing in mind that the dancer is not using the anatomical positions of the limbs exactly as found in a normal physique.

It is essential that the bones are kept in their natural alignment to each other, but because they are moved or kept in place by ligaments, tendons and muscles, the latter have to be trained to maintain that alignment, and each dancer must know and feel how to use the muscles correctly.

The teacher can see the superficial muscles working, but only the dancer can feel the deep muscles working. Therefore it is most important that every teacher understands how to guide her students and pupils towards a proper under-standing of the deeper muscles, because if a teacher sees a superficial muscle working incorrectly and the dancer feels no pain in the deep muscles, the pupil may be compensating for this incorrect use of muscles, and the stress that results could be in one of the joints or deeper ligaments. This stress can and frequently does cause minor and major injuries far away from the point of origin.

This book is an attempt to show how a chain reaction is set up and through which inter-related muscular fields it should pass to create both a beautiful and co-ordinated movement for above all, the muscles of the classical dancer must work in co-ordination if their movements are to have line, dignity, grace and musicality. e.g. If the leg is raised to the side above $90°$ and has to be held, one set of muscles is needed to move it upwards, but if it is held at some height, the co operation of several muscles is needed.

It is also written to help teachers to a clearer understanding of anatomical problems. Many children today are studying Human Biology at school and are therefore more knowledgeable about the uses and functions of their limbs etc. Many of the old commands given such as "Tuck your tail in", "Keep your back straight in an *arabesque*" are inaccurate and liable to misinterpretation because the laboratory skeleton demonstrates how impossible it is for anyone really to accede to such a request. As long ago as 1723 John Weaver, dancing master of Shrewsbury Grammar School realised the importance of relating the performance of dance movements to anatomy. Celia Sparger continued that work in her *Anatomy and Ballet* during the 1950's. I can only hope to further their pioneering.

Throughout this book I have preferred to use the common terms of the dancing and not the anatomy lesson, believing that neither teacher nor student needs yet another vocabulary of movement. Moreover as dance movements have to be "felt" as well as "thought", it is easier for the dancer to understand the everyday language in use, excepting those French terms which are the international language of classical dance.

I

STANCE

THE normal child of today rarely stands or walks with the spine fully extended unless he or she has had some form of strict physical discipline, therefore the muscles from the pelvic girdle to the waist are seldom brought into play or even into a state of tonicity (i.e. are ready to take part in any movement requiring some effort). Nor are the muscles within and above the rib-cage in a similar state, therefore the weight of the body is usually carried slightly sunken into the hips and, as he or she walks, there is a slight movement of the pelvis upwards and downwards as the feet are raised alternately from the floor and the weight of the body is transferred to the leading foot as it descends on to the floor. The classical dancer's walk is slightly different, (see p. 8).

The stance of the average healthy child of normal weight and proportions does vary a little from time to time, as growth can be erratic and a sudden lengthening of the body and/or limbs does affect stance and movement until such time as the child learns to accommodate his or her body to the greater length and weight required. The following points are a guide of what the teacher should look for in assessing their suitabilities as potential dancers.

Normal Stance

A child's natural stance is best studied by standing him or her still, weight equally distributed over the two feet pointing straight forwards, close but not pressed together.

Points to look for:

Front View. (figures 1, 2).

1. The face should appear centrally balanced over the breast-bone, navel and feet.

2. The shoulders are level. If they are not this could indicate a slight curvature, unequal growth or carrying a bag always on one shoulder.

3. The arms hang relaxed to the sides of the body. Note the relationship between the upper and forearms and the hands. Note how the arm is set in the shoulder; whether the elbow joint is inverted or everted; whether the palms of the hands face the same plane as the insides of the elbows; and whether the arms are of equal length.

4. The hips should be level. If they are not this could indicate some curvature of the spine or an unequal length of leg. The size of the hips seen in relationship to the knees and the proximity of the latter to each other indicates the angle at which the femurs are set into the hip-sockets. This in turn indicates to some extent the degrees of turn-out that could be achieved with training. If the hips are narrow, adequate turn-out is sometimes difficult.

5. The centre of the knees should be directly above the central points on top of the feet between the ankle bones, as well as directly under the nipples. If they are not, there may be some curvature or structural anomaly giving rise to knock-knees or bow legs.

6. The feet should appear to rest on the floor, the toes slightly and easily spread with the weight equally distributed over the metatarsal arch (i.e. between the big and little toe-joints and unseen heel). The muscles of the lower leg should be held so that the ankle bones are level and the insteps appear firmly controlled. If the feet roll inwards or outwards, or the toes cannot be directed forwards, there may be some structural anomaly giving rise to weak ankles, or insteps, or some type of tight tendon or ligament resulting in a sickled foot, or cramped toes; or there may be some irregularity of growth resulting in a long big toe, a second toe longer than the big toe, or a too short little toe.

Side View. (figures 3, 4).

The three major and natural curves of the spine should be clearly visible:
(a) The cervical, curving inwards towards the centre line.
(b) The thoracic, curving outwards from the centre line.
(c) The lumbar, curving inwards towards the centre line.
The fourth or sacral curve rounds under the buttocks.

1. If the child stands straight, a straight line should be seen to run through the body from the crown of the head to a point roughly at the centre of the foot. This indicates whether the weight of the body is being correctly distributed, or if it is too far behind or in front of the centre line of balance.

2. If the line of balance is correctly centred it should fall in front of the ear, through the centre of the hip-joint and knee to a point roughly in the centre of the foot. This can indicate if the child has a hollow back, sway-back legs, tight hamstrings or rarely, a short Achilles tendon.

3. The lateral side of the foot, particularly the heel and little toe should be seen to rest firmly on the floor.

Back View (figures 5, 6).

1. The back of the head should be directly centred over the spine, which should run through in an absolutely straight line from the axis to the sacrum. Whether the vertebrae are visible or not will depend upon how well the child is covered, but the line should always be visible, (diagram 1b).

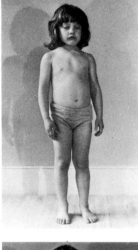

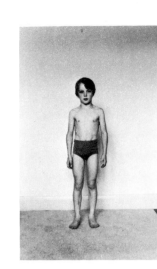

Normal Stance. Emma at 5 years compared with Mark at 10 years.

1   **Front View**   2

Emma was doubtful at being photographed and did not stand quite straight.

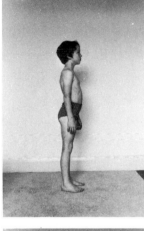

3   **Side View.**   4

Emma's baby tummy very much in evidence, together with typically arched back, but Mark's is fast disappearing.

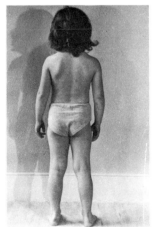

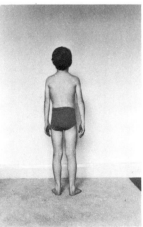

5   **Back View.**   6

Both children were a little worried at having photographs taken at this angle and did not stand too well.

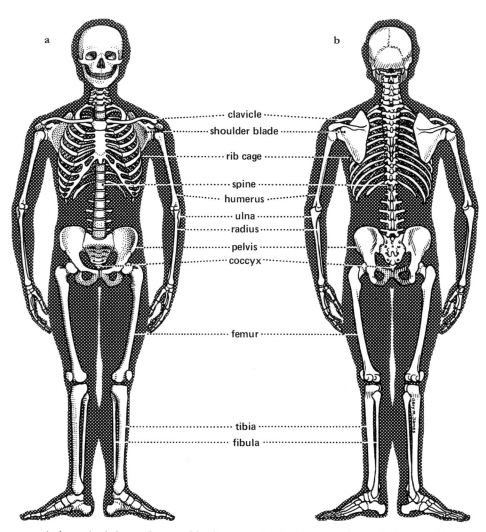

a   b

clavicle

shoulder blade

rib cage

spine

humerus

ulna

radius

pelvis

coccyx

femur

tibia

fibula

1   A dancer's skeleton, front and back views with feet in 1st and arms in *bras bas*. Note the seat of the turn-out.

2. The shoulders should be level and the shoulder-blades identical in size and shape. If they are not there may be some curvature, some discrepancy in growth, or weakness in the muscles on one side of the torso.

3. The waist line should be level, as should be the line of the hips. These should be equal in size, shape and equally balanced each side of the spine. If the hips and waist line are not horizontal to the perpendicular line of the spine there is some anomaly.

4. A straight line should be seen to run through the centre of each leg from the posterior superior iliac spine to where the Achilles tendon inserts into the heel. There is also a line running through the legs at an angle from the great trochanter,

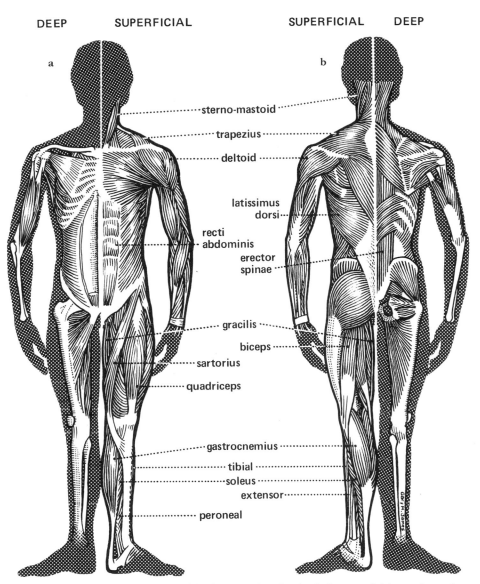

DEEP   SUPERFICIAL   SUPERFICIAL   DEEP

a   b

sterno-mastoid

trapezius

deltoid

latissimus
dorsi

recti
abdominis

erector
spinae

gracilis

biceps

sartorius

quadriceps

gastrocnemius

tibial

soleus

extensor

peroneal

2   A dancer's muscles. Front and back views showing both the superficial muscles and the deep muscles. Note the seat of the turn-out. Compare with figures 7, 8 and 10, 11.

through the femur to the knee and then straight on to the same point where the Achilles tendon inserts into the heel. The relationship between the angled and straight lines of the legs should be carefully noted. If the angle is acute there is a greater degree of knock-knees than normal; if obtuse, a greater degree of bow leg, which can appear at several levels; that just above the ankle being the most difficult to train for pointe work if it is excessive, (diagram 1b).

5

Before starting to study classical dance both teacher and child should understand the functions of the four parts of the body from which all movements emanate.

1. BONES are hard, solid parts making the human skeleton. In every normal child they grow from birth to maturity. The length of this period varies considerably. Although they cannot be stretched, with careful training in dance their relationship to each other can be slightly changed.

2. LIGAMENTS are the bands of fibrous tissue binding the bones together and – in general terms – holding the organs of the body in place. They also grow naturally and are inelastic. Their relationship to each other and the bones can be slightly adjusted by the muscles, they therefore require very careful handling.

3. TENDONS are the strong bands of tissue terminating or connecting the fleshy parts of some muscles. Some of these can be slightly stretched, but only before maturity.

4. MUSCLES produce movement throughout the body and are so intimately connected with all the parts that it is their function to keep bones, ligaments, tendons and muscles in their proper relationship to each other when any movement takes place. They grow naturally, but can be stretched, relaxed and developed, and so must be properly educated if the dancer is to obtain the best results from the turn-out, (diagrams 2a and b).

Balletic stance used in classical dance is not the abnormality believed by laymen. The turn-out is no more than a refinement of normal stance, which has to be maintained throughout a dance if the lines of the movement are to be made visible and shown in relationship to each other as the dancer steps and moves into and out of poses, jumps, turns and the rest.

When under exertion, as the classical dancer will be when maintaining turn-out and correctly carrying and transferring the weight of the body from one foot to the other, the inner- and outer-intercostal and accessory respiratory muscles, particularly the sternomastoid and trapezius (diagram 2) are used to control the movement of the cervical and thoracic spinal curves. All of these are attached to various regions of the ribs, sternum and scapula. It is therefore not enough to work on the leg muscles. Those of the entire body have to be trained. They have to be re-educated for classical dance and therefore the first essential is to achieve correct stance because so many injuries arise from an incorrect distribution of weight and muscular tension.

The very fact of turning-out without re-educating all the muscles of the body, particularly those above the hip-joints, merely throws the pelvic girdle forwards and the weight backwards, thus straining thighs, knees, ankles and feet as well as weakening the spine in the sacral and lumbar regions, which should be the strongest and firmest part of the body. It is in this region where the greatest strain of maintaining turn-out as well as most of the many adjustments in balance take place (diagram 3).

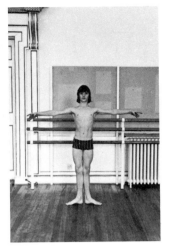

Classical Stance. Compare figures 1 – 6 with those of Susan and Stephen after 5 years' training and aged 14–15.

7   **Front View.**   8
Note larger stretch of boy's arms, with head held a little higher.

9   **Side View.**   10
Note girl's slightly more forwards stance.

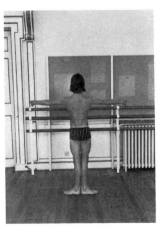

11   **Back View.**   12
Note straight line of both children's spines.

The effect of turning-out can be seen in the so-called "dancer's walk". In classical dance whenever walking is required, the hips are kept as still as possible, the knees over the toes, the weight of the body being carried directly over to the supporting foot from TOE to HEEL. However when a classical dancer walks in outdoor shoes the process is reversed. Through training he or she unconsciously maintains the position of the body used in the classical walk, but because of the heeled shoe, the weight is transferred from HEEL to TOE. So, whilst maintaining the classical posture, the weight is differently distributed and the dancer sways like a sailor when the boat is rolling in order to propel himself. The dancer tries to keep his weight more forwards, as he does when dancing, but his heels go down first instead of his toes. Thus it shows that to achieve and maintain turn-out the legs must be given technical freedom in the hip-joints, that is all the muscles in that area, if there is to be a semblance of normality. But the muscles must also be strengthened to be held at their new length.

Front View (figures 7, 10 and diagram 1a).

1. The head is centred, well-poised and seemingly relaxed but controlled by conscious effort.

2. The shoulders are level and opened outwards through the stretch of the arms, which are curved and held. They descend very slightly from shoulder to wrist and a straight line should be seen to run through the bones from the centre of the arm-pits to the middle fingers.

3. The rib-cage is lifted upwards from the waist, which is slimmed by the action of all the muscles in this area. The diaphragm is taut and only moves very slightly outwards and inwards with the intake and exhalation of breath. This causes the lower ribs to expand and contract slightly sideways.

4. The hips are level and face the same plane. The stomach is firmly held.

5. All the muscles attached to the pelvic girdle, thighs and legs are stretched or held in one way or another, so that the legs are turned-out from the hip-joints. A line should be seen to run straight through each leg from the upper margin of the hip-joint (i.e. the ascetabulum) to the ankle bones (compare figures 1, 4 with 7, 12). If the leg muscles are fully stretched, ideally there should be no gap between the legs from the crutch to above the knees, a small one between there and the top of the calf; and a longer, larger one between mid-calf and the heels.

6. The knee-caps, when seen in profile of a fully turned-out leg, should be flat, except in those cases (particularly boys) where children have prominent knee-caps (patellas).

7. The ankles should be well pulled-up so that the feet do not roll inwards or outwards, (i.e. the two malleoli of each foot should be level). There should be a clear space under the instep and a tiny one between the metatarsal arch and the balls of the big toes.

Side View (figures 8, 11).

1. The spine should be seen to be fully stretched upwards and downwards

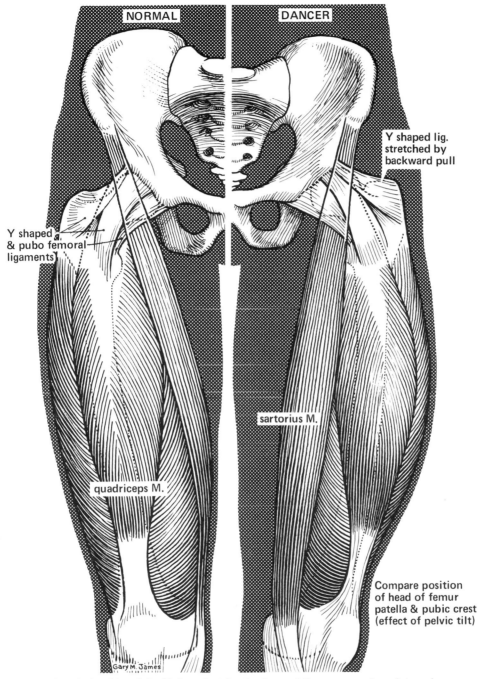

NORMAL   **DANCER**

Y shaped lig.
stretched by
backward pull

Y shaped
& pubo femoral
ligaments

sartorius M.

quadriceps M.

Compare position
of head of femur
patella & pubic crest
(effect of pelvic tilt)

Gary M. James

3   The relationship of the Y-shaped and pubo-femoral ligaments to the pelvis and upper
leg in a normal person and a dancer. Note the difference made to the lines of the muscles
by the turn-out.

from the waist, so that the three main shock-absorbing curves have been straightened as far as possible. The fourth or sacral works with the lumbar curve, (see below).

(a) The straightening of the cervical curve allows the head to be lifted and appear to balance and move freely without any movement taking place in the neck or shoulder girdle. The chin will not be "tucked in" nor held tense as this inhibits an easy head movement. It should be noted that more movements take place in the cervical region than elsewhere. It is essential that the freedom of the head to direct the eyes and control the ever changing balance of the body must be clearly understood.

(b) The straightening of the thoracic curves allows the shoulder-blades to flatten and glide over the rib-cage, which in its turn can be lifted more easily to hold the weight away from the legs. This straightening can allow the arms to move more freely in their sockets. A certain amount of movement is possible in the thoracic region of the spine, but this is always limited by each individual's physical structure and ability to move and control his movements.

(c) The straightening of the lumbar curve ensures that the spine from waist to sacrum is stretched straight downwards, which helps the muscles of the thighs and abdomen to achieve a greater degree of movement, and thus a greater degree of turn-out. As there is no movement in the sacral and little in the lumbar regions of the spine (the sacral vertebrae are fused together), it is vitally important to understand what little there is and how this part of the spine must be strengthened and controlled to keep it as still as possible. If it is not controlled and kept still the result is an arched and weakened spine with the accompanying loss of stability in all balancing movements.

2. No matter to what degree of turn-out the child has achieved, a straight line should be seen to run through the centre of the leg from the hip-joint to the middle of the foot and through the middle toes.

3. The toes should be stretched outwards and rest easily and evenly on the floor.

Back View (figures 9, 12 and diagram 1b).

1. The head is centred and easily posed.

2. The spinal column is straight and all the various parts of the torso are equally balanced on either side of the central line.

3. The shoulder-blades are well-opened and pulled apart. The shoulders (as in front view) are level, with the arms slightly descending from thence to the wrist. There should be no tension in the neck, across the shoulders, nor along the arms.

4. The waist line should be clearly defined. If lines are drawn at an angle from the arm-pits to the coccyx on either side, these ideally but rarely form an equilateral triangle. A slight movement sideways, inwards and outwards of the lower ribs and shoulder-blades should be visible to indicate that the student is breathing correctly.

5. All the muscles in the pelvic region from the waist to the hip-joints are seen to be controlling the uplift of the body as well as the drawing down and together of the muscles in buttocks and thighs.

6. A straight line should be seen to run through the centre of each leg from the posterior superior iliac spine to the ankle bone of the turned-out foot, and the spaces between the legs are the same as they were when viewing the student from the front.

7. The lateral side of the foot is usually level to the floor, but if the student is standing correctly, then it should be possible to see that the weight is carried over the heel and the ball of the little toe, (i.e. the outside of the metatarsal arch). (Compare figures 1–6 with 7–12).

To achieve this classical stance the student requires a chain reaction through all the muscles in co-operation from the tips of the toes to the crown of the head and vice-versa, and from finger-tips to finger-tips.

In general there is insufficient understanding of the use of spinal movements in classical dance. Instead of all the muscles, tendons and ligaments connecting the spine to the rest of the torso, or emanating from the spine itself being strengthened and made more flexible to get the best results from the turn-out, the spine is frequently stiffened. This inhibits most movements. Teachers should remember that the three natural curves of the spinal column must continue to act as shock-absorbers as they do in ordinary life. At all times they must take part in the whole movement, and thus be flexible if limbs and head are to be co-ordinated with the torso, and if muscular tension is to be eliminated.

The action of turning out sets up a chain reaction through all the muscles downwards from the waist to the toes, and upwards to the neck. It should be understood however that they do not all move with a similar action at the same time. A counter pull of forces is always necessary to maintain balance against the forces of gravity. This is vital, (see p. 14).

The action of turning-out the legs alters and narrows the shape of the base over which the dancer must carry or balance the weight of the body whether on one or two feet, (figures 41–51). When standing normally the body is balanced and the person can rock fairly easily to and fro from heels to toes without over-balancing. This area is determined by the length of the feet. But when adopting classical stance (i.e. the turned-out position) it is smaller, being only the width of one foot, therefore it cannot rock as a whole from head to toe. The straightening of the three curves allows the dancer to maintain a central line of balance through the spinal column to a point just in front of and between the two feet, or through the bones of one leg to just in front and over the instep of that foot. If he or she wishes to move the body to and fro, the movement can only take place from the hip-joints, the dancer's so-called "hinge". The body cannot move as a whole from toes to head. Thus, if the central line of balance is to be effectively maintained, then all the muscles of the torso should be drawn towards and round the central line. But because the dancer has to move through space carrying his or her weight, the limbs and head must be given as much freedom as possible where they join the

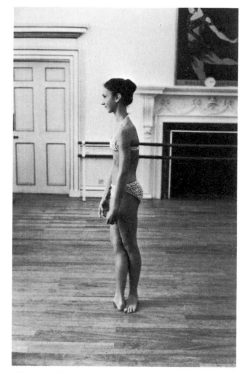 

The Re-Education of the Pelvic Girdle and Abdominal Muscles.

13 Judith has "tucked her tail in" with the result that she cannot stretch upwards and this has repercussions in the shoulder girdle.

14 Judith has fully stretched her spine when in a closed 4th to show how weight is centred between the two feet.

torso if they are to play their proper part in counter-balancing the body, whether it is stationary or moving. In the same way the three spinal curves must be made sensitive to the tiny adjustments necessary to achieve balance. The teacher's first task should therefore be to help students to use the spine correctly and loosen their arms and legs at hip and shoulder-joints and the head in the cervical region.

I. THE RE-EDUCATION OF THE PELVIC GIRDLE AND ABDOMINAL MUSCLES

The re-education of the abdominal muscles and those emanating from the lower spine is essential if the lumbar curve is to be strengthened. It is also necessary if those in the thoracic and cervical curves are to be similarly stretched, strengthened and made more flexible in order to balance and/or hold the torso over the supporting turned-out leg or legs.

There is insufficient understanding of how to use the muscles in buttocks, thighs and abdomen to pull the sacrum downwards and the rib-cage upwards when straightening the lumbar curve. By encouraging the student "to tuck the tail in" the muscles throughout the region of hips and abdomen are cramped rather than

12

held taut, making it difficult, sometimes impossible, to stretch upwards from the waist-line. This incorrect use of the muscles has repercussions in the shoulder girdle, (see p. 17 and figures 13, 14).

To ensure the greatest degree of turn-out within the limits set by the individual physique, the following is of use.

Stand with feet not turned-out nor pressed tightly together, bringing the lower half of the body into a state of tonicity by holding it correctly, lifting the weight of the rib-cage away from the abdomen and allowing the lungs to expand and contract easily by a proper use of the diaphragm and respiratory muscles thus giving space to stretch and re-educate the muscles of the hip-joints, (diagram 3).

1. Lift the rib-cage away from the waist line by breathing in to expand the chest and shoulders outwards and sideways.

2. Slim the waist by drawing inwards and stretching upwards the recti abdominis to their limits. These are the strong muscles of the body stretching from the front of the pelvis to the lower parts of the chest. They are encased within others, the fibres of which run in different directions and connect pelvis, lumbar and sacral vertebrae, lower ribs and thighs.

3. Draw the buttock and spinal muscles towards each other as well as towards the coccyx (i.e. tail). These are the gluteus maximus connecting the leg with the pelvis and, together with the biceps, give shape to the buttocks, and those muscles lying beneath as well as the lower part of the erector spinae, that large muscle which must also be stretched and strengthened.

N.B. The stretching and strengthening of the sartorius, gracilis and other muscles within the inside of both the upper and lower legs is more important than strengthening the quadriceps which is usually emphasized (see below). Without these muscles being fully extended and controlled the student loses contact with the floor because the heels do not rest there after descending from a jump or when transferring weight, particularly if he or she has a short Achilles tendon (see p. 14). Moreover it is the strong stretching of these muscles away from the body which adds the necessary length to any *arabesque*.

II. THE RE-EDUCATION OF THE MUSCLES OF THE KNEES, LOWER LEGS AND FEET

Having

1. Lifted the rib-cage;
2. Slimmed the waist;
3. Drawn the buttock muscles inwards and together, and
4. Turned the legs outwards from the hips,

the dancer must now ensure that the muscles leading to and within the knees both in the upper and lower legs are also stretched, strengthened and re-educated to keep the bones in proper relationship to each other now that the base on and over which they work has been narrowed by the turning outwards of the legs at the hip-joints, (figures 7–12).

5. Pull up the rectus femoris in order to flatten the patellas, i.e. the centre muscle of those forming the quadriceps which straightens the knee at the front of the leg.

Those with sway-back legs must be taught not to stretch the muscles inserting behind the knee (i.e. the ham-strings) so far that the patellas are drawn backwards and the legs away from the perpendicular. Together with those having average straight legs they can achieve this straightening if the muscles comprising the quadriceps are stretched upwards and at the same time, the sartorius and gracilis are stretched downwards. Both sets of muscles are used in this way to allow the buttock muscles to be drawn together. But it can only happen if the weight is carried correctly forwards over the centre of balance.

6. Stretch the sartorius downwards diagonally between the outer edge of the thigh to where it folds round just below the knee on the inside of the leg. This is the longest muscle of the body and is influenced by the shorter gracilis which stretches from the front of the pelvis under the sartorius to the knee on the inside.

Far too little attention is paid to the sartorius and gracilis which play a vital part in maintaining turn-out, (see second para. 9 below). The former stretches diagonally between the outer edge of the hip-socket and the inside of the knee and is in great need of re-education. Once the leg is turned-out, it should be continually stretched and relaxed always with the same action and in the same direction with every stretch and bend of the legs in order to keep the bones in proper relationship with each other. On its proper action depends the closing of the feet accurately in 1st, 3rd or 5th positions, when the weight of the body must be firmly replaced over the two feet.

7. If the rectus femoris is pulled upwards to straighten the patella correctly, the other quadriceps muscles also pull upwards from where they emerge at the knee to where they insert into the hip-joint.

It is the counter pull of forces between the sartorius, helped by the gracilis and the quadriceps, upon which the turn-out largely depends. The action of the sartorius being pulled downwards and the quadriceps upwards allows the Y-shaped and pubo-femoral ligaments more space in which to move and thus the head of the femur to rotate very slightly outwards in the hip-joints. But the head of the femur can only be held in this new position if the quadriceps are pulled upwards and held by the strong inwards pull of the buttock muscles, (see diagram 3, and pp. 15 and 109).

N.B. The two parts of the Y-shaped ligament run upwards from the outer and inner edges of the great trochanter of the femur to where they join and insert into the pelvis just below the anterior superior iliac spine. The pubo-femoral ligament lies between the great trochanter and the pubic bone. The two ligaments thus control, to a very great extent, the "tilting" of the pelvis forwards and backwards as well as the turn-out.

8. Pull on the soleus and gastrocnemius which give shape to the calf downwards into the Achilles tendon to counter the upwards pull on the ham-strings and

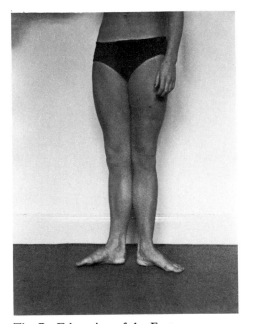 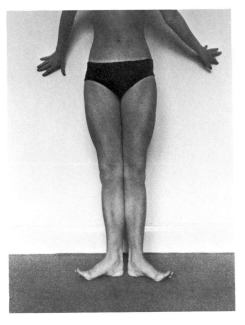

The Re-Education of the Feet

15 Susan has over-corrected her R. foot, the metatarsal arch is not fully on the floor. Compare with L. foot and leg and note shortening of muscles on the inside of R. leg.

16 Susan showing the three points of balance across the metatarsal arches and heels.

quadriceps (i.e. the former include the biceps and other muscles at the back of the thigh whose tendons stand out behind the knee). The action of the calf muscles inserting into the Achilles tendon together with the tibial, peroneal and extensor muscles of the lower legs controls the movements of the ankles, insteps and toes, and must be used in such a way that the ankle bones (malleoli) are kept level and the heel is firmly placed on the floor. This levelling of the ankle bones is essential because it determines the angle of the talus (i.e. weight bearing bone, see p. 30) as it is tilted when the dancer rises through the foot. These muscles also control, with others, the entire action of all the bones forming the two arches of the foot upon which the entire weight of the body is rested by the talus.

The stretch of the sartorius downwards influences the upwards stretch of the calf muscles, thus countering the downwards stretch of the ham-strings and giving more strength to the Achilles tendon and those muscles leading to and through the ankle. All are needed to keep the whole foot firmly placed on the floor and in correct alignment with the tibia and fibula, (i.e. the bones of the lower leg).

9. Stretch the muscles under and over the feet outwards towards the toes so that the bones are straightened and held in proper relationship to each other, particularly those in the ankle and instep.

If the weight of the body is held correctly all the muscles under and on top of the feet can be stretched outwards, particularly if those on both the inner and outer sides of the calf and ankle, and under the instep are equally controlled and held in a state of tonicity.

Because so much depends upon the correct action of the sartorius and gracilis, teachers must guard their pupils against the over-correction of a "rolling" foot. By over-correction these and the tibial, peroneal and extensor muscles cannot be stretched or worked to their fullest. In fact they are usually shortened and weakened because the weight of the body ceases to be carried over the three points of balance of the feet. Instead it is placed too much on the outside of the feet so that the muscles are over-stretched and throw the weight backwards. This weakens the turn-out either because the buttock muscles cannot be drawn together easily; or if they are, the "tail is tucked in" shortening muscles in the upper legs, thus inhibiting a strong movement upwards of the abdominal muscles. In addition the over-correction distorts the line of the foot and thus displaces the talus, (figure 15).

Students can quickly feel the counter pull of all the leg muscles if they stand correctly with feet in 1st position and consciously try to turn their toes upwards from the metatarsal arches, keeping the balls of the big and little toes and heel firmly on the floor. These are the three points of balance on and over which every dancer must work when on one or two feet, placed flat on the floor, (figure 16).

It is when performing this movement that teachers can help to correct the footwork of those dancers whose feet naturally sickle outwards from the ankle, either because of some discrepancy in the bone structure, or because the muscles on the inside of the foot are longer than those on the outside. By bringing the foot alone inwards from the ankle until its centre line is seen to be directly under the centre of the knee, the outside muscles can be slightly stretched and those on the inside better controlled and strengthened, provided the student is able to keep the malleoli (ankle bones) of each foot level with each other.

It is not so easy to correct those students whose feet tend to sickle or curve inwards. This may be due to natural bone structure or short tendons, ligaments and muscles on the inside of the foot, in particular the peroneus longus which leads from just below the knee down both sides of the leg and inserts on the outer side of the instep or foot. But the act of slightly stretching all the muscles on the inside of the leg to bring the central line of the foot under the centre of the knee can help further stretch and strengthen the sartorius as well as all the muscles round the talus (see pp. 30, 31). This slight adjustment can also help to correct what is a slightly bowed leg.

A dancer's foot is the most important part of the body to be brought into and kept in a proper state of tonicity during the first stages of training. The accuracy, quality and speed of all footwork depends upon how it is used and/or held momentarily as the dancer moves and transfers his or her weight, adjusting the arms, torso and head to the varying demands of balance, step and pose. The highly complex relationship of ligaments, tendons and muscles within the ankle, instep and toes is described later (see p. 34), because these are in a constant state of change with the transference of weight. Nevertheless when practising classical stance correctly the student must attempt to hold the feet evenly on the floor. The

16

toes should be straight and comfortably stretched outwards from ankle and instep. The amount of space to be seen under the instep varies considerably because the muscles under some feet can be so sensitive and flexible that they all but touch the floor when the foot is relaxed, but react immediately to the slightest stimulus or change of balance. On the other hand there can be a large space if the student has tight tendons and ligaments, which can prevent the foot working at all easily because it is so difficult to stretch the muscles. This is particularly the case with those students possessing the aesthetically admired "high instep". They have to work twice as hard as those with an average instep. The fact that pointing the foot requires little or no effort often means that the student neglects or is unable to use the muscles under the foot correctly. These are usually tight because the bone structure, ligaments and tendons are such that the dancer cannot even feel the stretch outwards from both under and over the insteps and toes.

Before starting work upon the re-education of the muscles of the body above the waist line, the teacher should realise the length and extent of the movement within the three curves of the spine, which give the best results when they have been straightened (diagram 4). But they must be kept flexible if the dancer is continually to centre his or her weight round the central line of balance. The straightening of the lumbar and sacral curves has been described (see p. 10). It indicates how little can be done to increase movements in this area. Because the five sacral vertebrae are fused together and the transverse processes of the fourth and fifth lumbar vertebrae curve slightly upwards, most spinal movement takes place from the third lumbar vertebra, that is from and mostly above the waist line. What little takes place below this point is due to the action of the various muscles pulling the sacrum and coccyx downwards in the process of turning out and the slight tilt of the pelvis when the leg is raised sideways above 60° or forwards when moving into an *arabesque*. It should therefore be the dancer's aim to keep the lumbar region as still as possible, because "rocking" the pelvis to and fro by continually arching and jerking the spine straight only weakens and places great strain on the inter-vertebral discs at the waist line and on the sacro-iliac joint. This spoils the line of the back, particularly if children are told "to keep the back straight in *arabesque*".

III. STRAIGHTEN THE THORACIC SPINE

Having stretched the turned-out legs so that the knees are flattened and the feet firmly placed, the weight of the body will have been brought more forwards with the flattening of the lumbar curve. The spine must now be stretched further upwards from the waist by straightening the thoracic curve, i.e. from just above the waist line to the base of the neck. It is important to note that the lumbar vertebrae, having been slightly adjusted with the pulling down of the pelvis, have influenced the stretching of the eleventh and twelfth thoracic vertebrae.

10. Lift the rib-cage a little further upwards by stretching the thoracic vertebrae strongly erect. The child should feel that it is being lifted from underneath by the recti abdominis, thus eliminating the "baby tummy" (figures 1–6).

17

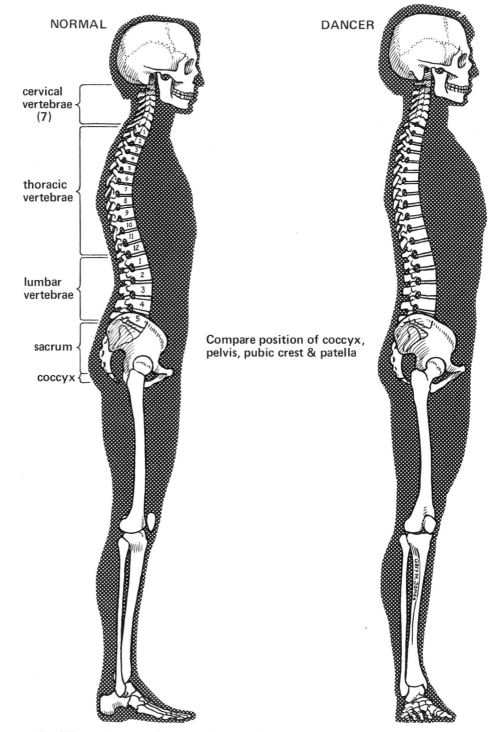

NORMAL

DANCER

cervical
vertebrae
(7)

thoracic
vertebrae

lumbar
vertebrae

sacrum

coccyx

**Compare position of coccyx,
pelvis, pubic crest & patella**

4   The difference between the spine of a normal person and a dancer. Note the difference in the line of the spine and the tilt of the pelvis through the turn-out.

11. Free the rib-cage from weight by expanding the ribs with an intake of breath. This should press them out sideways so that the arms feel they also are being opened outwards and away from their sockets, as much by the intake of breath as by the strong stretch upwards and outwards of the latissimus dorsi and trapezius muscles connecting the spine to the arms, shoulders and head. The latissimus dorsi are a complex series of muscles controlling and connecting the movements of the pelvis, lower spinal vertebrae with the arms. The trapezius controls and connects the movements of the upper spine with the arms and head.

The thoracic curve is capable of more movement than the lumbar because the muscles connecting these vertebrae to the rest of the torso are kept constantly at work by the natural inhalation and exhalation of breath. In many children studying classical dance however, the rib-cage protrudes because the breast-bone (i.e. sternum) is thrust upwards and forwards by the way the shoulders are pressed backwards towards the spine and rib-cage. Never allow a child to "press the shoulders back until you can hold a pencil between them". As mentioned above, the shoulders can be stretched outwards with the straightening of the thoracic curve. This gives the intercostal muscles controlling the movement of the lungs within the rib-cage more space. Moreover as these and the accessory respiratory muscles connect the shoulders and head intimately to the entire rib-cage, diaphragm, pelvic girdle etc (diagram 2), the important part they play in the movements of the torso cannot be stressed too often.

After stretching the thoracic vertebrae well upwards from the waist, the student should be able to curve the body forwards either along the whole length of the twelve vertebrae in co-ordination with those of the lumbar and cervical curves; from the seventh for a deep bow; or from the fifth where in conjunction with an inclination of the head, that gracious bow performed by the ballerina can be attempted. These vertebrae can also be curved backwards if they have been stretched upwards before attempting any kind of back bend or *arabesque*, and similarly curve or bend from one side to the other, or even rotate the bent body round from front to side, back, side and front again before recovering the upright position. All three bends and the circling are possible of performance with very little movement taking place in the lumbar region, provided the weight is correctly centred over and upwards from the legs, and the waist is kept slimmed, (see p. 56, figures 80–87).

Perhaps the most important function of the fully stretched thoracic curve is during an *arabesque*. As the working leg rises upwards or is stretched outwards from a *développé*, the pelvic girdle tilts forwards thus extending the fifth and fourth lumbar vertebrae in the same straight line. To counterbalance this forwards and downwards pull, only the slightest movement can take place in the other lumbar vertebrae, therefore the thoracic vertebrae play a vital part in stretching the rest of the spine and head upwards towards the central line to give this pose its beautifully curving shape. Most of this curve takes place from the seventh thoracic vertebrae upwards. But it can only happen if the accessory respiratory and shoulder muscles are in no way inhibited by the shoulder-blades being pushed into the rib-cage, (figures 17–22).

The Re-Education of the Lumbar, Thoracic and Cervical Curves
The straight line of the spine compared with the curved line needed for an arabesque.

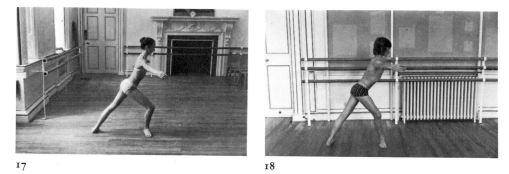

17 18

Compare Judith's more lyrical straight line with Stephen's masculine stronger line.

19 20

The fully stretched but curved spine, weight well forward, but boy's not quite so far as girl's.

21 22

Judith now increases the forwards tilt of the pelvis and stretches outwards. Stephen shows the line through his spine and the stretch of his shoulders.

A stiffening of the thoracic curve which thrusts the breastbone upwards and forwards, also causes that common fault of tension across the shoulders, usually followed by an awkward use of the arms. Many children fail to lift or use their arms freely from the socket. The belief that the shoulders should not move at all in classical dance is erroneous. It is anatomically impossible to raise the arms above shoulder level without some movement taking place in the muscles of the shoulder girdle. Nevertheless the shoulder bones can be held calmly at the same level no matter how high the arms are raised, provided the latter move freely within and are stretched away from the sockets, the neck is fully extended and the head too moves independently. And, finally, provided the fundamental rule of classical dance is not broken, that the arms are always curved except in *arabesque*. If the arms are raised straight upwards this can be achieved if the shoulders are opened widely from the chest before being raised and the arms continue to follow the straight lines of the bones from the centres both under and over the shoulders to the middle fingers of the hands, (figures 23–30).

However it is not enough to stretch and make the thoracic curve strong and flexible if students are to lose tension across the shoulders and gain freedom to move the arms freely in their sockets. It is important to note that some muscles lying under the shoulder-blades insert into the spine just where the ham-strings emerge. The so-called ham-strings are the large tendons rising from the back of the knee connecting the biceps, femoris, gluteus maximus and medius with those muscles of the lower leg and sacro-iliac joint, that vital part of a dancer's pelvis where only the tiniest movement should be allowed to take place. If therefore the weight of the body is pushed downwards by the pressure of the shoulder-blades on the rib-cage, the stretch of the ham-strings is impeded because the weight is too far back on the heels. The important muscles in the pelvis and thighs are cramped. i.e. The latissimus dorsi muscles, which arise from the great spinal muscles and stretch upwards underneath the scapula to the arms cannot work, (see p. 19).

Similarly if the movement of the lower ribs is impeded either by an arching of the spine at the waist, or a "tucking under" of the lumbar and sacral vertebrae, it is impossible for the recti abdominis to stretch upwards and help raise the rib-cage, whose muscles must equally stretch outwards and sideways, and relax inwards if the shoulder-blades are to be kept calm whilst breathing. It is vitally important to ensure that the shoulder-blades glide outwards and inwards OVER, and NOT ON the rib-cage, and are held comparatively at the same level by the action of the muscles under, at and round the socket as well as those attached to and under the ribs and breast bone. The freedom this gives to the arms can only be exercised if the student is taught to use the triceps correctly. The three heads of this muscle insert under and into the arm socket and are intimately connected with the latissimus dorsi, trapezius and other muscles vital to breathing. Too often the effort of holding the arms correctly with the insides of the elbows and palms of the hands facing the same plane means that the muscles above the arm (i.e. the deltoid etc) are raised

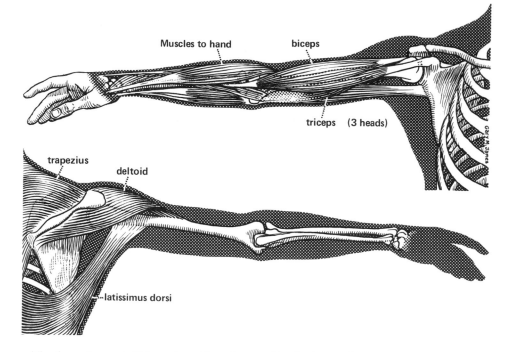

Muscles to hand   biceps

triceps   (3 heads)

trapezius

deltoid

latissimus dorsi

5 The dancer's arm held in 2nd position, front and back view, indicating the need for correctly using the latissimus dorsi, deltoid and trapezius muscles.

and rolled forwards, which not only puts strain across the shoulders but also narrows the chest, (diagram 5).

The teacher can help a child to feel how to use the triceps muscles as well as breathe correctly and freely by placing the fingers flat on the base of the child's shoulder-blades. Then, as the child breathes in, gently press the blades slightly outwards and apart so that the rib-cage expands easily and naturally as the shoulder-blades open sideways. The slight pressure also helps to prevent shallow breathing in the top of the lungs if they are impeded in any way by tension across the shoulders or by a raising of the breast-bone caused by pinching the shoulder-blades backwards.

Another very important aspect demonstrated by the slight pressure of a teacher's fingers to flatten and open the shoulder-blades is to help a child understand how to move the arms almost independently in their sockets as they close from 2nd to 1st, rise to 5th, descend to 2nd position and lower to *bras bas* and vice-versa. If the entire torso and head are fully stretched, but not taut, it should be possible for all save those children with prominent scapulas to draw a circular line with the minimum amount of movement occuring in the bones of the arms and shoulder, because the muscles both over, under and inserting into the shoulder-blades are doing their work correctly (figures 31–34).

Having now balanced and counter-balanced the many muscles that hold the body upright against the forces of gravity, the student now reaches the final stretch of the neck and head to give line and direction to the dance.

12. Free the muscles holding the jaw so that the chin is neither "poked out", nor "tucked in", i.e. in particular, the sternomastoid and trapezius which, if tensed, restrict breathing; the former constricts the wind-pipe, the latter the inter-costal muscles and thus the lungs.

13. Raise the crown of the head straight upwards from the base of the neck, straightening the cervical vertebrae. At this point the central line of balance should again be checked to ensure that it runs from the crown of the head through the centre of the body to a point just between and in front of the turned-out feet when in 1st position facing front (figures 35, 36).

The greatest degree of spinal movement takes place in the cervical region, i.e. the seven cervical vertebrae where so much tension can appear if young dancers strain to hold their arms correctly, (see p. 22). Teachers should make students understand that by straining across the top and back of the shoulders they distort the lines of the arms and inhibit the independent movements of the head, as well as prevent the lifting and curving of the thoracic and cervical vertebrae in any type of movement taking place throughout the torso. Just as a straight line should be seen to run through the legs from the hip-joints to the ankle bones of the well turned-out feet, so should straight lines be seen to run through the centre of the arms slightly downwards from the armpits to the middle fingers. If the neck is not pulled upwards to free the shoulders, this cannot happen.

It is perhaps not too ridiculous to suggest that if it were not for the strong ligaments, tendons and muscles such as the sterno-mastoid and trapezius tying the head on to the torso and linking it to the arms etc: the head could swivel round independently above the atlas. Yet despite these strong links between the head and torso, the student must realise that the head is capable of much independent movement, whilst the neck muscles play a vital part in colouring and giving subtle details, allowing the head to indicate the line to be followed by the dancers (figures 37, 38).

One of the simplest ways to help stretch the cervical curve upwards to its fullest is for the teacher to place the palms of the hands over the child's ears so that the thumbs rest just behind and the pads of the fingers press gently underneath. Then, insisting that the child keeps the feet firmly on the floor, gently try and lift him or her upwards so that the neck muscles and cervical vertebrae are felt to stretch upwards very slightly. Too often children, particularly when growing and if shy, fail to stretch the head upwards and hold it when making use of the flexibility of the spine in this area.

Once children can feel this stretch, they should be encouraged firstly to keep the head and shoulders still and try to bend the neck forwards and sideways, and

23

The Re-Education of the Shoulder Girdle.

23   **24**

Compare Susan's more curved arms when both stand correctly with arms in 5th position.

25   **26**

Compare incorrect 5th positions. Susan has raised her shoulders, but Stephen has shortened one arm.

27   **28**

Compare the upwards stretch of both boy's and girl's arm held correctly in 5th position.

The Re-Education of the Shoulder Girdle.

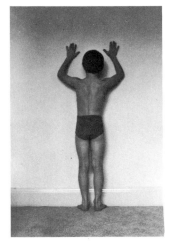

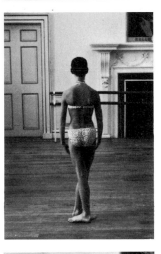

29 **30**
The untrained Mark has to
bend his arms to keep his
shoulders down. If he
stretches his arms, his
shoulders rise.

31 Judith has opened her
shoulder-blades sideways,
held her arms and poised
her head correctly.
Judith has not bothered **32**
to stretch upwards.

33 The arms held **34**
correctly in 2nd
position. Shoulders
flat and opened side-
ways as in figure 31.
The arms are
too far behind the
shoulder line, so that the
shoulder-blades
cramp the spine and
prevent the waist from
being slimmed.

roll it from side to front and the opposite side. Secondly to move the head independently by keeping the shoulders and neck still whilst turning, inclining and then lifting it to the side, dropping it to the front and lifting it again to the side.

If they understand how the neck and head can move independently of each other, they can be helped to realise the importance of co-ordinating the neck with the head if the latter has to move backwards. It is quite possible to drop the head backwards without neck movement at all if the chin is directed straight upwards to the ceiling and not allowed to poke forwards. It is also possible to curve the cervical vertebrae backwards without moving the head, provided the chin is not "tucked in". But this movement can be uncomfortable – even painful – if these vertebrae are not fully stretched upwards before they are curved backwards with head fully erect (see figure 39, 40 and p. 63).

Both these independent movements are used in classical dance, but it is more usual and more natural to co-ordinate the movements of neck and head, and the degree required for each depends entirely upon the type and quality of movement performed. In all such movements there is a moment when the head must be firmly controlled and given no freedom to relax. For example when performing a simple back bend with one arm raised in 5th position (i.e. just in front of the shoulder): the head is first lifted, eyes looking into the raised elbow, it begins to move backwards as the cervical curve increases, but just after the stretching and curving movement begins to take place in the thoracic curve, the head should be controlled and held in position. The moment when the head must be controlled depends very much upon the length of the child's neck and the shape of the shoulders. If it is allowed to relax and drop further back, it will cause pain across or in the shoulders and neck. The child may then relax quickly and jerk the head upwards only to cause pain in the throat or across the chest.

VI. A RE-APPRAISAL OF CLASSICAL STANCE

Where should a teacher begin to stretch the child when he or she moves into classical stance? Should it be the feet, or at the head? The fore-going discussion began with the centre of the body. That is with the pelvic, lumbar and thigh regions in order to emphasize the difference between the normal and the more sophisticated classical stance, which requires a turn-out of the legs from the hip-joints. The legs were then discussed downwards to the feet before dealing with the rest of the torso and head. But to adjust the entire body to classical dance requires a simultaneous reaction and co-ordination of stretching and controlling all the muscles of the body. It is not enough for the teacher to demonstrate, physically correct or give orders for this or that adjustment. Such commands are often misinterpreted because they are insufficiently explicit. But more often because neither pupil nor teacher understands the full implication of so simple a demand as "keep your back up".

If there is to be an immediate reaction to the command "Prepare" as the introductory music begins, then both teacher and child should know how to

The Re-Education of the Neck Muscles.

35 The cervical spine and head are well poised and stretched so Judith looks alert. **36** Judith again has not bothered to stretch upwards.

37 Compare figures 37 and 38 and note subtle change of line given by slight alteration of the head. Judith looks straight at raised arm and has slightly curved her spine backwards. **38** Judith has slightly inclined her head and looked into raised arm, but curved her spine slightly forwards. Note the line of the straight spine.

39 Judith has bent the head alone and kept the cervical vertebrae fully stretched. Unfortunately Judith **40** has lost control of her head and could hurt her neck.

think for themselves and direct attention to their individual physique and make it react to its own capacity for movement within the rules of classical dance.

The response to a command "Prepare" should be instantly recognised, in the words of John Weaver, dancing-master of Shrewsbury Grammar School, who produced the first ballet d'action (1717); "The Face may not improperly be termed the Image of the Soul. . . . Every Passion of the Mind is discovered in the Countenance". He then discussed in his *Anatomical and Mechanical Lectures on Dancing* (1723) the function of the eyes. They must always convey "Meaning and Connect with the Object", whether it be the line of dance, colleagues on the stage, or the audience. The fourteenth point in achieving classical stance correctly therefore must be:

14. Focus the eyes correctly at all times.

When standing correctly the eyes should focus straight ahead and if the child is consciously thinking and working on what is to be performed, his or her thought will give life to the expression. Thus the command "Prepare" should result in an immediate stretching and controlling of the entire body because the child's brain has alerted his or her physical apparatus, which spontaneously reacts to allow him or her to reach the height indicated by the eyes, (figures 20, 21, and 37, 38).

VII. THE BODY IN MOVEMENT

To achieve classical stance thus aligning the limbs, torso and head over a much smaller base than in normal stance therefore requires a strong stretch and control equally over all the muscles. But to perform a simple dance movement may require considerable re-adjustment of those same muscles. Some may even have to function very differently by relaxing, stretching still further, or even contracting. Once correct stance becomes habitual and the child moves easily to take that stance, he must apply himself to the more important and difficult task of making the necessary muscular adjustments to perform any kind of dance movement.

One of the simplest yet best examples of this reversal of muscular function is when performing a *demi-plié*, where relaxation in every part of the leg from the hip-joint downwards is vital during the descent. Nevertheless the spine has to be kept stretched and controlled because it is the weight of the body which presses the knees downwards and outwards over and in the same line as the feet. When descending still further into a full *plié*, because the child has reached the full extent of movement in all the joints involved, the pressure of this weight causes the heels to rise, and only when it is impossible to descend still further must the dancer actively begin to stretch the leg muscles to help the ascent by pushing the weight of the body upwards. The spine is still held stretched and controlled as at the beginning of the movement, (see also p. 51).

It is when performing this movement at the beginning of the first lessons that the child begins to understand the vital difference between an active and a passive movement, and how the muscles will always react to some stimulus if the dancer wishes to remain on balance. In a *demi-plié* the weight of the descending body is controlled and held in place by the stretch and strength of all the spinal, abdominal and shoulder muscles to keep the vertebral column as straight and still as possible. But the ascending movement is determined by the gradual stretch and strength of all the leg muscles, those in the torso being kept held firmly controlled as it is pushed upwards in the same way as it was when descending. In both *demi-* and full *pliés* all the muscles on both sides of the body must work equally. It is when the child has to balance or transfer weight from one leg to the other that far more attention has to be paid to the function of the muscles in first one and then the other side, which must work in absolute co-ordination if the turned-out legs are to defy the forces of gravity and the dancer remain upright.

2

WEIGHT BEARING

SINCE the nineteenth century when danseuses interpreting the roles of sylphs and wilis began to dance *sur les pointes*, audiences have expected them to dance silently as befits these ethereal beings, unlike those performing folk and character dances whose footwork can vigorously accent the rhythm of the steps. Silent classical dancers unfortunately often fail to use the floor as a firm base, a spring-board from which to begin their dance. In so doing they neglect to stretch their leg muscles sufficiently strongly. This means that some part of the foot loses contact with the floor too early in the preparation and this weakens the action of the legs. i.e. children when training seldom bring sufficient pressure on to the whole foot during the preparatory *plié or fondu* before the moment when the weight of the body has sunk so far that it gives impetus to the whole foot to react, and all the muscles from heel to toe through the leg to the hip-joint respond and stretch upwards to propel the body into the air, either into a simple *relevé* or jump. It should be remembered that any step BEGINS with the preparation and NOT AFTER.

This failure to use the floor as a spring-board, together with a stiffening of the spine usually results in a displacement of the central line of balance, because if there has been some inequality of movement or weak pressure during the relaxation and push out of the preparation, there is bound to be some distortion or tension somewhere in the torso, shoulders and/or head. This prevents a maintenance of balance, and causes an unsteady descent into the *demi-plié* or *fondu* because the child has failed to relax all the leg muscles in the reverse order. Such faults occur even during a simple jump in 1st position (figures 130, 131) possibly because the buttock muscles have been clenched to maintain turn-out, or the toes clenched to grip the floor, instead of relaxing and then stretching again in the same direction and with a reverse action as at the beginning of the movement, whilst the spine is held erect to keep its upright position over the central line of balance.

The pressure and use of the foot (feet) in its relationship to the bones of the leg is of special importance because the weight of the body rests over the talus, unique in being the only bone of the leg to which no muscles are attached. The muscles hold it in place. Its function is to link the foot to the leg and transmit the weight of the body as the dancer moves from one foot to the other as in normal life. It is the keystone – as it were – on which the leg bones rest over the arches of the foot no matter which of the seven dance movements it is performing. It is therefore essential always to keep the talus accurately balanced over the two arches (i.e. the longitudinal and transverse, see diagram 6) no matter to which height the foot

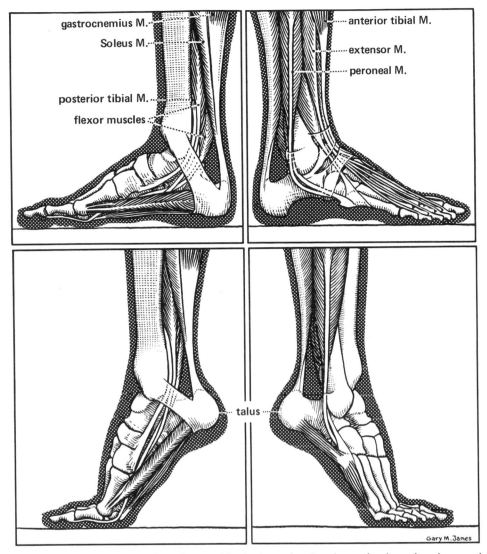

Labels on the illustration:

gastrocnemius M.
Soleus M.
posterior tibial M.
flexor muscles

anterior tibial M.
extensor M.
peroneal M.

talus

Gary M. James

6 The muscles of a dancer's foot, front and back views, showing the need to keep the talus exactly balanced no matter to which height the foot is raised. (The Talus is unseen, but its position is indicated.)

rises, and to ensure that the body is held so that its weight is equally distributed over the area of balance.

I. BALANCING THE WEIGHT OVER TWO FEET

It is useful to examine the area of balance over which the child must work when studying classical dance. The photos of Susan's feet (aged 15) after five years' training show both her footprints and the varying positions of the feet. The measurements disclose that the higher the dancer rises the smaller the area over

31

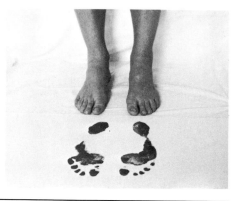

41 Susan standing normally. Size 3 standard shoe, medium fitting.
From heel to toe: 8".
Across metatarsal arch: 7".

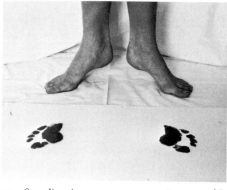

43 Standing in 1st on quarter *pointes*:   14½".
Across one metatarsal arch: 3".
Spread across toes of one foot: 3¼".

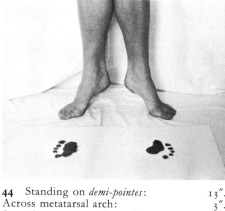

44 Standing on *demi-pointes*:   13".
Across metatarsal arch: 3".
Spread across toes of one foot: 3½".

47 Standing in 5th, feet flat, from little toe back to big toe front: 9¾".
Across two metatarsal arches: 6½".

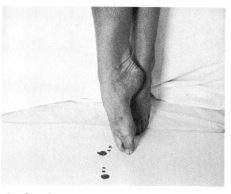

48 Standing in 5th full *pointes,* i.e. overall width across toes: 5".
Spread across toes of each foot has increased from 1⅝" in 1st, to 1⅞".

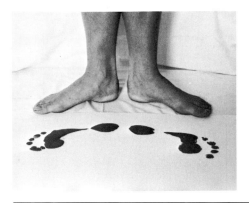

42 Standing in 1st from 2nd to 2nd toe: 16″.
Across one metatarsal arch: 3″.
Across one heel: 1½″.
Overall area is roughly: 16″ × 4″.

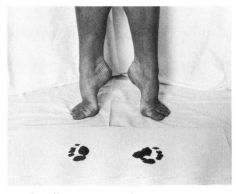

45 Standing on 1st on three-quarter *pointes*:   10″.
Across and just above metatarsal arch: 2½″.
Spread across toes of one foot.   3½″.

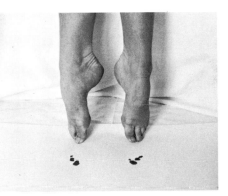

46 Standing in 1st on full *pointes*: 6½″.
Between little toes: 5½″.
Spread across toes of one foot: 1⅝″.

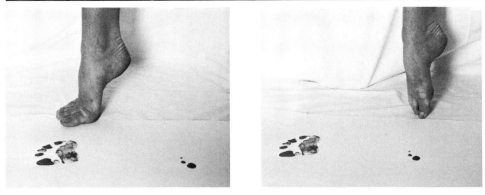

49   **50**
Shows that when Susan stands on *demi-pointe* one foot only, the spread across her metatarsal arch increases to 3¼″ (3″ when on one foot). When on full *pointe* the foot is not so turned out and the area is a mere 1¼″ × 1″.

33

which to balance and control the entire body. They also disclose that the smaller the area, the more the toes spread to take the weight and when standing *sur les pointes* the legs often turn slightly inwards from the hips to keep the balance centred through the bones of the legs, talus and three major toes.

The measurements given are worth studying as they may help teachers to realise the amount of strength and understanding of muscular control a child should acquire before attempting to dance *sur les pointes*.

N.B. Measurements are included in the captions to figures 41–50.
When Susan stands on *demi-pointe*, one foot only, the spread across her metatarsal arch increases to $3\frac{1}{4}''$. ($3''$ when on two feet). When on full *pointe*, the foot is not so turned-out but the area is a mere $1\frac{1}{4}''$ by $1''$, (figures 49, 50).

It needs much hard work on the rest of the body as well as the feet and legs before any child can stand so firmly centred over the feet and legs at any height. Compare Susan's photographs (figures 42–45) with those of Emma aged five (figures 51–58) trying to balance on *demi-pointes* without any training. Although she possesses an unusual sense of balance for so young a child, in her efforts to hold her weight steady she makes the same mistakes as many older students after four or five years' training, because, like them, she has not understood how to equalise and counterbalance the stretch and action of the various leg muscles in order to keep the talus correctly centred under the leg bones and over the arches of the feet no matter to which angle it has been tilted (diagram 6).

The angle to which the talus is tilted and held is controlled by all the muscles of the ankle and foot. These must be trained to stretch and relax very accurately. The child should know exactly how and when to hold the feet at quarter, *demi-*, three-quarter and full *pointe*, and realise that at each position when raising the heel from the floor extra stretch and control is required above hip and waist level as well as within the toes, insteps and ankles. This extra control is needed because the metatarsal arches slope backwards towards the heel from big to little toe-joints, and if the child attempts to keep the little toe joint on the floor, the big toe joint will lose contact with this base, thus the talus will not be resting firmly over the arches, (figure 53). To counteract this the child may decide to grip the floor with the toes, (figure 54) by tensing the muscles in the sole of the foot which affects the calf muscles and results in a slackening of the quadriceps, then of the abdominal muscles and a forwards bend from the waist in order to centre the weight more firmly. Or it can lead to an arching of the spine because the chest has been protruded in an attempt to centre the weight. There are numerous other incorrect ways of re-adjusting balance because the talus has been displaced, but they only weaken the work of the feet and legs, and can ultimately lead to groin or back trouble.

Some understanding of the girl's difficulty in rising through the feet on to full *pointe* may be grasped by comparing the photos of Emma's first attempts to rise on the *demi-pointes* with those of the ten-year old Mark (also untrained, figures 59, 60 and figures 133, 134). It will be noted that he has risen straight on to his *demi-pointes* at the first attempt because he has moved forwards on to his toes, kept his

34

knees straight and his spine erect, thus ensuring that his weight continues to be balanced over the central line from the crown of the head to rest over the two feet.

Comparison between the boy's and girl's positions, (figures 133, 134) also shows to some extent why boys in general find it easier to rise on *demi-pointes* than girls, particularly during the first stages of training and with the onset of puberty. Boys never have to carry the extra weight of bust and buttocks that the girl always acquires when she develops (see p. 98). By the age of eleven the boy's spinal and abdominal muscles are usually stronger than those of a girl because by the age of eleven-twelve and certainly by thirteen-fourteen most girls have begun to put on extra weight in the pelvic girdle and bust, and this unfortunately is mostly fat and bone, not muscles.

Susan's footprints reveal a well-proportioned, mobile foot, but because it is highly arched there is apparently little difference between her *demi-* and three-quarter *pointe*. However the measurements show that the space between her toes lessens as she rises and the photos demonstrate how much further she has stretched all the muscles of her legs so that the weight remains equally distributed over and through the centre of each foot. Thus as the talus has been tilted further downwards by the action of all the muscles in instep and ankle, it has been kept accurately balanced under the leg bones and over the two arches. This becomes clearer if the photographs of the two (figures 42–48) and the one foot (figures 49, 50) are compared. It will also be noted how much more stretched are all the muscles when poised on one leg and how the centre lines of the leg bones and that of the foot rise absolutely perpendicular to the floor.

N.B. As sometimes happens Susan's feet, like Emma's, are not identical in shape, In figure 48 it appears she has slightly sickled her foot, but the foot-print shows her weight is correctly centred.

II. RISING THROUGH THE FEET

It is when rising through the feet to the full *pointe* that the greatest care must be taken to ensure that the downwards stretch of one set of muscles is countered by an equal stretch upwards of others. This equalisation is necessary because the talus must remain firmly centred under the leg bones and over the arches of the foot as it is tilted downwards by the lifting of the heel. If required by a choreographer, a trained dancer can rise *sur les pointes* with knees bent (figure 132), but in so doing is careful NOT to turn-out the legs, and keeps the spine and weight firmly controlled and centred so that the knees protrude well in front of the body – somewhat in the same way that the untrained Emma managed unconsciously when rising to the *demi-pointes*, (figure 56). This demonstrates a child's ability to keep the body controlled whilst performing isolated movements requiring a relaxed knee but a stretch of the muscles in ankle, instep and foot. It is also required in the daily *pliés*.

However children are not required to perform such movements when training. Instead they have to be taught to rise through the foot (or feet) turned out at an

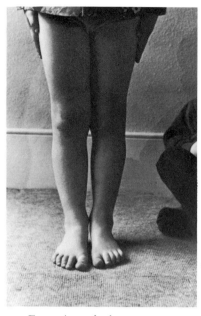

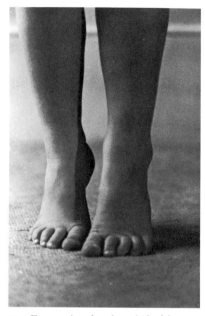

51 Emma is ready, but toes are not quite level and weight is a little too far back.

52 Emma rises but has shifted her L. foot a little forwards so has cramped her toes and also gone over to the R. little toe.

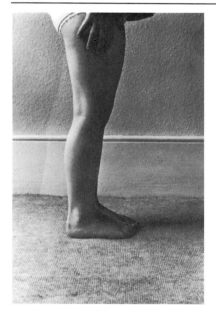

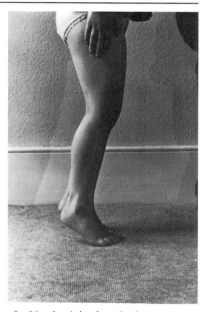

55 Let us try sideways.

56 Nearly right, but the knees are not fully stretched.

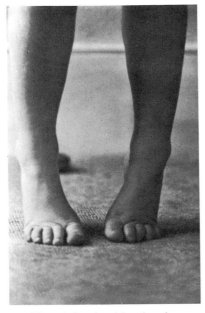

53 Has tried to level her feet, but sickled outwards!

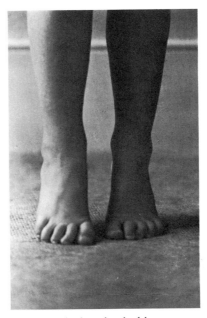

54 Now she has clenched her toes.

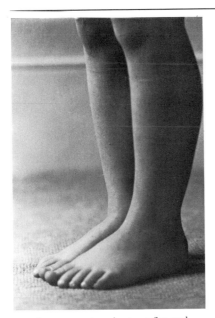

57 Let us start again, toes flat and level, weight a little forwards.

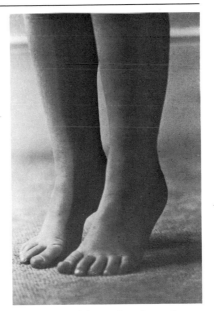

58 At last! After an hour's work.

37

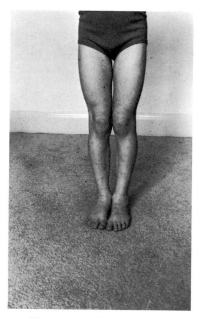

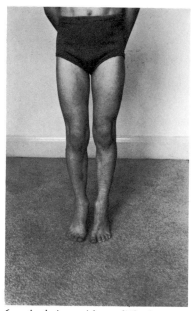

59 The untrained Mark stands correctly.

60 And rises without difficulty. Note how his toes are kept well stretched.

angle determined by the action of the muscles in the hip-joints and pelvic area some distance away from the feet where the major part of the rise takes place. It is now that those muscles crossing from one side or part of the limb or torso to the other come into play to help the dancer to balance, (see also p. 66).

The child should stand correctly, fully stretched with feet in 1st position and without slackening any control in any part of the torso and legs, particularly the knees, try to push the weight of the body gradually upwards by increasing the stretch and/or tightening of all the muscles from the hip-joints to the toes. None work in isolation. All are continually at work, but their order of importance changes very slightly as the talus begins to tilt.

1. Help the heels to rise a little by drawing all the buttock muscles tighter towards each other and attempt to keep the insides of the upper legs together. This helps to bring the weight a little further forwards and upwards if the sartorius and gracilis are well stretched downwards and the quadriceps upwards (figure 43, quarter *pointe*).

2. Push upwards moving the weight towards the metatarsal arches by lifting the muscles in the insteps and round the ankle. All these muscles continue upwards into or round the knee and help to stretch still further the tibialis posterior and anterior, the gastrocnemius and soleus (diagrams 2 and 6). These in their turn

also help to keep the talus in its correct relationship to the femur as it tilts further downwards. But only if these muscles play an equal part with those holding the talus over the longitudinal and transverse arches. The teacher can ensure this by seeing that the malleoli (ankle bones) of each foot are level (figure 44, *demi-pointes*).

3. Pull all the muscles under the insteps and heels still further upwards and lift the heels over the metatarsal arches. This will involve pulling and tightening the calf muscles still further upwards and stretching downwards all those inserting below or in front of the knee. This extra tightening should cause the quadriceps and through them the abdominal and buttock muscles to react and similarly stretch still further upwards. Moreover because the upper parts of the legs are a little further apart, the weight is balanced centrally over an angle made by the two straight legs and will have moved very slightly forwards (figure 45, three-quarter *pointe*).

N.B. It is at this point that the teacher should insist that the weight of the body is firmly centred and the line of balance runs through the centre of each foot. If the talus is incorrectly tilted and its natural angle in relationship to the bones and arches displaced, the weight will fall either on the big or little toes. This can cause damage. If it falls on the big toe it may ultimately result in a bunion (i.e. halus vulgus). If it falls on the little toe, it can lead to painful peroneal and tibial muscles and sometimes stress fractures.

4. Simultaneously stretch and/or tighten all the muscles already named and with a quick intake of breath, spring or rise ideally to the tips of the three big toes, but the exact number depends on the shape of the individual foot. This little spring or calm rise requires the strength of all the muscles in the whole foot to tilt the talus to its limit. This can only be done if the muscles lying under the instep are tightened to their limit (figure 46, full *pointe*).

It is easier to rise from 5th position because the weight is centrally balanced from the commencement of the rise. The legs are kept in close contact throughout and the slight pressure and stretch of the various muscles against each other helps the child to stabilise balance (figure 48). This is very valuable later when the child has to be taught to glide the toes of the front foot very slightly towards the back foot during the rise, and away during the descent in order to keep the legs tightly closed. (Susan has done this in figures 42–48). This tiny movement also helps the child to realise how small a spring is needed for a true *relevé sur les pointes* (see p. 34).

This same movement also demonstrates the need always to replace the weight firmly over the two feet when closing in any position no matter to which height the working leg or the supporting foot has risen, nor at what speed the step has been performed, nor whether the movement is to be repeated or not, (figure 61). It is when closing on a *demi-* or full *pointe* that the student must be advised to give an extra lift to the torso from the waist to keep both legs fully extended. If this is not done, the working leg is often shortened in the hip-socket (figures 62, 63) thus displacing the pelvis, so that if the weight is to be transferred from one leg to the other, the dancer is no longer in complete control, and will lose both the line of the step and the balance of the body.

39

Something similar to this centralising of weight during a rise in 5th position should occur when the dancer moves from 1st to *pointe tendue devant* or *derrière*. As the working foot glides outwards to its fullest extent, the toe should reach exactly the same spot it would have reached if it had moved from 5th. This slight movement inwards occurs because the working leg should be so turned-out and stretched that the tiny adjustment in weight over to the centre of the supporting leg can be achieved smoothly. Moreover if this is not done and the *pointe tendue* is a preparatory movement for some balancing exercise, the adjustment of balance then necessary to bring the weight over the supporting leg can easily result in a loss of control of the spine, the line of the working leg or a displacement of the hips (figures 64, 65).

III. TRANSFER OF WEIGHT FROM ONE FOOT TO THE OTHER

If all the leg bones and muscles are kept in proper relationship to each other when the legs are turned-out and the body held correctly (figures 7–12), it is comparatively easy for a child to balance over the area proscribed by the two feet in both the open and closed positions. The next step is to ensure that the child understands how to maintain that relationship during the descents and ascents of the *demi-* and full *pliés*, perhaps continuing upwards with a further stretching of the feet and insteps into a rise or jump. If so, this rise or jump should be followed by yet another relaxation through the whole leg, and finally another stretch to gain correct stance. The teacher should also insist that there is a proper relaxation and stretch of all the appropriate muscles before any child attempts to transfer weight from one leg to the other.

The first of such attempts is best made if the child stands correctly in 1st position and raises one foot into low *retiré*. It is now vital to hold the supporting leg and body firmly controlled as in stance but, by relaxing the muscles at the hip-joint and knee, lift the working foot lightly pointed from the floor. If this is done slowly the child will realise how it is possible to hold the supporting leg firmly stretched and controlled, whilst relaxing parts of the working leg, provided there has been an adjustment of balance to bring the crown of the head over and just in front of the instep of the supporting leg. If the working foot is raised from 5th position, only a tiny adjustment is necessary because the weight is already centred (see p. 39). But even this small lift of the working leg cannot be achieved smoothly if there has been any slackening of control in all the muscles of the torso above the hip-joint to the head on the supporting side (figures 66–69 also p. 46).

It is perhaps important to insist that a completely controlled relaxation and/or stretch of the appropriate muscles takes place before any attempt is made to transfer weight from one leg to the other through an open position. To perform the simplest transfer i.e. *chassé à terre*, the child should ensure, when making the preparatory *demi-plié* that the weight is centred equally over both feet, but at the moment when the heels might lose contact with the floor, the working foot resists the pressure. Instead it pushes outwards, the whole foot firm on the floor to direct the leg forwards, sideways or backwards to one of the open positions.

40

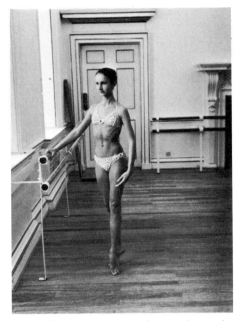

61 Judith standing correctly on *demi-pointes*, weight equally balanced over two feet.

62 Judith has not returned correctly to 5th and has shortened her front leg, thus displacing the hip line.

Weight-Bearing

63 An incorrect pass through 1st position during a *rond de jambe à terre*, throwing the weight on to the supporting leg and spoiling the centre line of balance.

41

During this movement the weight of the body should remain firmly centred between the two feet because the knees, although bent, are controlled at the same level as the one leg slides outwards. It is only when the correct open position has been reached that the transfer begins to take place. This happens as the weight of the body is pushed in the required direction by the new working leg stretching to *pointe tendue*. If this is to be successful then the maintenance of an erect spine is essential because the body, led by the head, should always be carried directly over to the new supporting leg before the completion of the transfer so that the head is seen to direct the movement and anticipate the final pose or position (figures 70–74).

In all such transfers of weight through *chassé à terre*, even without a preparatory *demi-plié*, it is valuable to see no child moves into too large an open position. If it is too large it is impossible to guarantee that the new supporting leg will stretch directly upwards and be perpendicular to the floor as the new working leg stretches to *pointe tendue*. Moreover if the position is too large the child will find it difficult to hold the weight away from the waist and firmly centred. This is why every child should realise the exact stretch of its own leg as the foot slides from a closed to an open position and relate that space to the stretch of the leg in *pointe tendue*. If they do this correctly, they can control the size of their *chassé*. The exact half-way point at which the transfer begins is determined by the size of the completed *chassé* outwards when both knees are equally bent in a good *demi-plié*. The depth of the *demi-plié* is determined by the amount of relaxation in the child's leg muscles. It is of no value to try and increase the depth of the *demi-plié* by failing to press the heel along the floor. The inside of the leg, particularly the heel leads the movement and without that firm pressure along and then out of the floor, the muscles of the legs will not be able to complete their full stretch as the weight of the body is passed from both to one foot.

An easy way to ensure that a child can hold the weight of the body away from the waist during any transfer of weight is to teach him or her how to breathe correctly. The following is a guide to use when moving from two to one foot, one foot to two, or from one to the other.

1. Breathe in at the moment of transfer because the body is made lighter when the lungs are full, thus the new working leg is better able to work against the forces of gravity to push the weight upwards and over (e.g. *chassé à terre*).

2. Breathe in during those movements when the balance of the body is being adjusted so that the spine is freed as far as possible from weight as the head, arms and working leg move from one position or pose to another (see pp. 81, 82).

3. Breathe in at the moment when the foot (or feet) leaves the floor in any kind of jump and hold the breath whilst the body is in the air, exhaling only as the leg (or legs) swiftly, but in due order descends into *demi-plié* or *fondu*, (e.g. *sissonnes*).

4. Breathe in when rising from the *demi-plié* or *fondu* into a *relevé*, *pirouette* or *tour* and hold the breath until the supporting heel (or heels) reaches the floor (figures 127–130) then exhale as the working foot moves from the *retiré* into some

The Result of Over or Under-Crossing

64   65

Stephen has over crossed and Judith has under-crossed in *pointe tendue derrière*, with the result that both students' hips are out of line when the leg is lifted.

pose or position. When the *pirouette* moves directly into a pose from the preparation e.g. *attitude*, breathe in as the working leg moves into the pose simultaneously with the rise or *relevé* into the turn.

If the breath is taken in correctly in all the above circumstances the waist is kept slimmed, the rib-cage firmly held upwards and expanded sideways so that the lumbar and thoracic vertebrae are given room in which to adjust themselves as the dancer moves into a new pose or position. This adjustment may only be a minor one, as happens when the weight is directly transferred as in *chassé à terre*. But it may require a major adjustment as in *grand rond de jambe en dehors* where the dancer must tilt the pelvis forwards as the leg moves from side to back and straighten again when moving from back to side *en dedans* (see p. 82 and figures 112–119). Moreover as the pelvis is tilted forwards so the spine has to be extended further outwards and stretched upwards (see p. 20), and when moving *en dedans* the dancer has to recover the upright position as the leg passes from back to side without any sinking into the hip on the supporting side.

43

It is not only by the correct transfer of weight and breathing that a child learns to combat the forces of gravity. When the normal child begins to walk Nature provides natural counter-weights to keep the body upright. These are the arms which give classical dance its first important rule of balance; THE LAW OF OPPOSITION. "Always use the opposite arm to leg whether it is working or supporting". But in day to day movement this implies that the child only moves forwards. If he moves backwards Nature provides the second important rule for classical dance: THE LAW OF NATURAL ÉPAULEMENT, interpreted by Noverre as: "Always brings the same shoulder forwards as foot remaining in front, whether it is working or supporting". This means that in daily life the child tends to turn the body towards the foot moving backwards, because that is the foot which ultimately takes the weight of the body.

As children grow and explore their capacity for movement, they then begin to use a third rule applicable to classical dance: THE LAW OF COUNTER-BALANCE. "Use the counter-balance of arm and/or leg to keep the body upright when first attempting to balance on one leg and defy the forces of gravity". A particularly valuable rule when trying to hold one leg out sideways, e.g. with left leg raised, the right arm held in 2nd and the left arm moving into 5th position, thus the raised left leg is counter-balanced by the right arm, the left arm helping to keep the weight of the body centred over the perpendicular right leg.

It should be noted in classical dance, as in the three natural laws of balance, the hips and shoulders are kept square to the same plane if the arms are to do their work properly. Thus the second law suggests there is still a fourth law of natural balance. As the child moves backwards there is a deliberate change in the direction of the body whilst the eyes remain focussed on a particular point. The child is attempting to move backwards in a straight line without turning the head to see where he is going. This natural reaction thus leads to the fourth rule of classical dance: THE CORRECT FOCUS OF THE EYES. "Always focus the eyes correctly to give direction and line to the movement", (see p. 28).

Keeping the hips and shoulders square to the same plane is of the greatest importance during the first years of study as well as an understanding of the need always to synchronise the movements of the arms with those of the legs. This need of synchronisation arises from the nature of the muscles, because of the way they link limbs, torso and head together and keep them moving. Most children readily understand the relationship of the part to the whole limb and can easily bend or stretch a leg or arm inwards and outwards in a straight line. They can also lift or lower leg or arm at some angle to the body. But the hinge-like movement at the hip-joints is not so easily accomplished when the legs are turned-out, unless the Y-shaped and pubo-femoral ligaments are given room to move by the stretching, strengthening and controlling of all the muscles in the hip-joints. This happens because the hip-joint is a ball and socket joint and the head of the femur has to be rotated outwards and held by the muscles of the buttocks before the pelvis can form part of the hinge (see p. 14). It is these latter muscles which are so

66 Judith has correctly stretched her spine and centred her weight with a slight tilt of the pelvis as her working leg is raised as high as possible.

67 Back view of 66. L. shoulder a little strained.

68 Judith has failed to keep her spine straight, thus the supporting hip is displaced.

69 Judith has "tucked in" the working leg at the hip so that she twists towards it.

difficult to control because they are invisible and must never be so tightly drawn together, or the coccyx pulled too far underneath, that they are incapable of further movement. If they are so clenched and unable to move, the child will not understand that this ball and socket joint, like that of the shoulders, is the main spring from and through which all the circling movements of arms in legs in classical dance must depend as well as many other movements. The reason for this is that although many muscles can be said roughly to follow the straight lines of the bones e.g. the quadriceps, triceps etc. – which have to be stretched and strengthened so that the dancer gets the greatest benefit from their length both before and after the limbs have been bent at some angle or another – it is from those other muscles which stretch from one part or side of the torso or limb and insert or cross from one side or part to the other which are in greater need of education. This is particularly the case with those inserting into or emanating from the ball and socket joints of hips and shoulders. The student must know not only how to use the muscles to maintain turn-out at the joint itself, but how to move leg and arm within their sockets so that they can also achieve freedom to cover space and give breadth to the dance (see p. 78).

V. WEIGHT BEARING ON ONE LEG

It is when all forces have to be gathered round the central line and be balanced over one leg that the dancer has to concentrate on more detailed ways of moving, particularly if the working leg has to pass through several positions before descending; also, as in many adagios, when changes are made in the line of the supporting leg as well as the body. The former is still controlled, as in stance, but the weight is now centred through the bones, therefore the muscles have to be held more firmly whilst those on the working side can be used differently. e.g. in a *retiré* those on the supporting side are fully stretched, but those round the hip-joint, knee, ankle and foot on the working side are stretched and/or relaxed as far as the hip-joint. Those above must hold the leg correctly turned-out so that if the dancer is to perform a *développé*, the leg can be unfolded at the correct height and angle without disturbing the balance on the supporting leg as some of the latter's muscles come into play to hold it in place. (see p. 69.)

It is now that the student must put into practise not only the four natural laws of balance, but also those fundamental rules of classical dance, which cannot be repeated too often.

1. Whether the leg is working or supporting it is turned-out at the hip-joint and the pelvis is kept as still as possible (see p. 20), remembering that once the working leg rises above 20° at the back or 60° at the side (a good average) the pelvis has to tilt to a greater or lesser degree, therefore it is important to feel that both legs are fully extended outwards as far as possible from the hip-joints.

2. The spine is held erect but flexible, and when necessary plays some part in the line of dance, e.g. when moving into an *arabesque* (see p. 17), or when helped by the head to direct the body into the line of dance, e.g. as in *sissonnes* (figures 123–125).

46

Chassé à terre

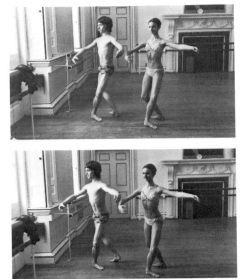

70 The *demi-plié* after the *chassé* forwards from 5th, weight between two feet.

71 The transfer forwards begins, body and head already anticipating the final pose *en avant*.

72 Completed transfer. Students are not in the same alignment in order to show central line of balance at the front and side of their bodies.

73 The transfer backwards begins, body and head have already anticipated final pose *en arrière*.

74 Completed transfer.

47

3. The hips and shoulders face the same plane and are kept as level as possible. There are exceptions, e.g. in certain *ports de bras*, or if the dancer falls into a lunge from a *développé à la seconde* at 90°, it is impossible to follow the line of the working leg downwards if any attempt is made to keep the shoulders level, as they are when falling forwards from *développé avant*.

4. Neither the working nor the supporting leg must be over-crossed, over-turned, nor over-corrected, nor must the working foot be sickled (figures 64, 65). A central line of balance must be seen to run through the bones of the supporting leg, no matter to which height it rises or sinks. Thus when in *fondu* the central line is seen to run through the spine and rest over the instep of the supporting foot, (diagram 7). Similarly a central line should run through the raised leg. Too often attempts are made to force turn-out by thrusting the heel forwards and upwards. This displaces the talus and has repercussions on the supporting side because the muscles of the working leg are twisted from ankle to hip-joint. This affects the muscles in buttocks and abdomen, all of which work together to maintain turn-out. This means that either the supporting leg twists towards the raised leg, or the "tail is tucked in" pushing the pelvis forwards so that the recti abdominis cannot stretch upwards (see p. 20 and figures 103, 104–106, 107).

5. The arms are always kept rounded except in *arabesque*. They are extended outwards from their sockets, but not allowed to move behind the body. If either is allowed behind when first working at the barre, the child soon acquires bad habits. Shoulders are immediately affected if the accessory respiratory muscles are impeded by any strain in head, neck or arms, (see p. 21 and diagram 2).

6. Always co-ordinate most carefully the arm movements with those of the working leg when balancing over the supporting side. It is often best to close the arms in 1st position than drop them to *bras bas* when moving the working leg from one pose to another either through *retiré* or *battement balancé* from front to back through 1st position and vice-versa. Pausing momentarily in 1st helps the child to stabilise balance by recovering an erect spine, because the rib-cage is freed from weight, the lungs can expand more easily as the leg passes through to its next pose (see p. 19).

7. Always maintain a free head movement. The brain orders the whole body. The head directs the line of dance, provided the eyes focus correctly (see p. 28). Because of the extra stretch in the classical dancer's spine the focus point should be just above and beyond the hand outstretched forwards at shoulder level, (figures 20, 21). If the eyes are focussed on the hand, except when specially ordered, the cervical vertebrae are not fully stretched and this affects the outwards stretch of the arms from the shoulders and then the thoracic vertebrae. This happens because the head is one of the heaviest parts of the body, its smallest adjustment can often help a child to recover balance. This is particularly important when studying an *arabesque*, when the forwards tilting of the pelvis often upsets balance if the head does not lead the thoracic and cervical vertebrae forwards, upwards and then slightly backwards towards the central line of the supporting leg. This occurs

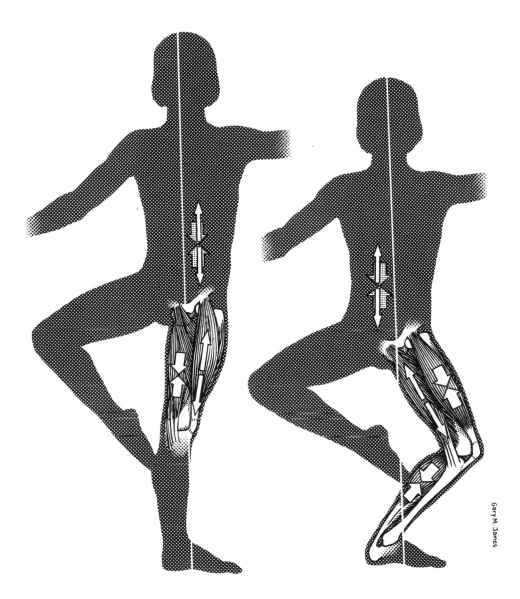

Gary M. James

7   A dancer's leg muscles in action when standing on one leg and when in *fondu*. Note the centre line of balance running through from the crown of the head to the instep and the counter-balancing of the muscles when the leg is straight and when it is *fondu*. See also figures 75, 76.

simultaneously with the raising of the working leg upwards also towards the centre of the curve, which should lie directly over the perpendicular supporting leg. Moreover it is the movements of the head, inclining, bending and turning freely which gives impetus and direction to all dance steps (see p. 25 and figures 37, 38).

3

CHAIN REACTIONS

In 1723 when John Weaver named his four movements of dance he was dealing, in broad terms, with those of which the muscles are capable. He stated that bending, stretching, rising and turning "are to Dance as Light and Shade are to Painting". Later, in 1760, Jean-Georges Noverre named seven movements, i.e. to bend, stretch, rise, jump, glide, dart and turn. However, he was not so concerned with the anatomical and functional aspects of movement, although he discussed suitable and unsuitable physiques. His main interest lay in defining the varying qualities of the dance steps. Therefore, when studying the mechanics of dance, one turns firstly to Weaver and later to Noverre, because Weaver's students needed to acquire anatomical knowledge when they took over the ballet stage from amateur courtiers, whilst Noverre's dancers, after professional training, began to develop expression as well as technique.

Although all muscles play some part in every step, even though passive, the students should understand the impetus given by the sheer weight of the body and its placing which makes the muscles react appropriately and moves this weight against the forces of gravity. It is only careful muscular discipline that gives quality to the dancer's line as he or she performs the seven movements, and it is by constantly changing the relationship of those seven movements that the student is helped to acquire the calm, ordered and elegant grace demanded from all who aspire to be classical dancers.

It has often been said that too much emphasis is placed in training the legs for classical dance, however it is true that the *demi-* or full *plié* plays a vital part in practically every step. It is important firstly therefore to analyse how a chain reaction is set up through the legs because the sophisticated movement caused by the turn-out requires that the body is brought slightly more forwards in a straight line from head to feet in order to place the weight over the natural centre of balance, otherwise the straightening of the spinal curves can throw the weight behind the feet. This is quickly seen if the turn-out is attempted without stretching the spine upwards from the hips.

BENDING AND STRETCHING

On analysis there are three bends of the legs as there are three of the arm, head and torso, all of which must be brought into play in some part of a dance or another if the dancer is going to be anything more than an automaton.

    1. The foot bends upwards towards the front of the lower leg at the ankle. It also stretches downwards away from the ankle.

    2. The lower leg bends backwards towards the upper leg at the knee.

    3. The upper leg bends towards the front of the abdomen at the hip-joint. Any other leg movement requires a stretching, raising or rising, turning or circling of one or another part. Moreover, whilst it is true that a *plié* relaxes some muscles in the areas between the joints, it also passively stretches others.

I. THE CHAIN REACTION IN A *PLIÉ*

It is well to remember that when any *plié* begins from correct stance, the legs are extended to their fullest and are taut as well as being turned-out from the hips. Therefore the chain reaction is more complex than the "heels raise, knees bend" of physical education. The most important links in the chain take place within or round the joints where the muscles and tendons from one side or part of the leg counter-balance those on the other to ensure, if done correctly, not only that the bones of the leg, knee and foot are kept in proper relationship to each other, but that the weight is held and centred through the legs – although they do not give it full support throughout the movement.

To feel how the chain reaction works, relax all the muscles below the hip-joints, holding those above firmly controlled. Place one hand over the muscles on the upper leg and feel how gently they are being stretched once they lose the taut-ness required to hold stance. It occurs as those at the back are reduced in length by relaxation. Or place the hand just above the ankle and feel a similar stretching behind whilst those in front of the ankle relax. Thus, if the legs are gradually bent at hip-joint, knee and ankle the chain reaction, starting from the hip-joint, passes through and stretches the quadriceps to where they insert into or below the knee. It then crosses and continues downwards, stretching particularly the Achilles tendon behind the lower leg. Some calf muscles terminate in this tendon. Other muscles and tendons emanating from above or just below the knee relax, particu-larly the tendons peroneus longus and brevis, the tibialis anterior and the extensors digitorum. But others also holding the talus in place, such as the tibialis posterior and tendo calceneous stretch as the heels leave the floor. From thence the chain reaction continues through the insteps to the metatarsal arches, where the muscles under the foot push the toes outwards a little as they bend at the joint and the weight of the body is balanced over the feet and not the entire leg (see diagram 6).

During the ascent the chain reaction is reversed. The muscles which have been passively stretched by the relaxation of those in the opposite sides or parts of the leg and foot must now play an active part as those others are gradually stretched and returned to their normal length, because the weight of the body has to be pushed upwards and replaced firmly over the legs. This requires a greater effort than the descent.

As the heels are pulled downwards to the floor, the chain reaction commences when the muscles under the instep relax and slightly stretch those above to shorten some ending in the Achilles tendon. The peroneus longus and brevis, tibialis anterior and extensors digitorum return to their normal length with the straightening of the foot and knee and bring the talus back to its normal position (i.e. foot flat to the floor). Because of the turn-out, this straightening must be reinforced by the action of the sartorius stretching between the hip-joint and knee, counterbalancing the action of the quadriceps at the front and gluteus maximus at the back pulling the leg upwards. At the same time the gracilis and buttock muscles inserting and/or connecting with those above the hip-joint also pull together again and finally push the body erect. During this final stretch upwards the dancer must concentrate upon controlling all the muscles holding the spine, particularly in the sacral and lumbar regions so that the weight of the body is properly replaced and centred above the hip-joints and over the two legs.

It is this final extension of all the muscles from the toes to the hip-joints and onwards through the spine to the head that distinguishes the dancer's stance from that of the normal person.

During the first lessons the descent and ascent during a *plié* should always be given equal timing so that the counter-balancing of muscles is a continuous process. A *plié*, no matter how small, and particularly if very deep, should never be sustained. It is always dangerous to wait if the weight of the body has sunk so far that the forces of gravity take over because the talus, resting on similarly tilted longitudinal and slightly spread transverse arches and toes is taking the entire weight of the body. The bones of both the upper and lower legs have been freed from that task.

II. THE CHAIN REACTION IN A *FONDU*

A student should always understand the purpose of each exercise. Many have several uses in which, on analysis, subtle differences must be made in performance if the desired results are to be obtained. One is the important differences to be made between the bend and stretch of a *plié* and that of a *fondu* (see diagram 7). In *plié* the line of balance is centred from the crown of the head to a point midway between the two feet no matter from which position the *plié* begins. Moreover both legs are equally responsible for lowering and raising the body. However when descending into *fondu* much greater care must be taken to centre the line from the crown of the head through the body and through space to where it rests over the instep of the supporting foot (see diagram 7). It is essential that the subtle change of weight mentioned above takes place BEFORE the *fondu* begins, no matter from which position. It is more usual for *fondu* to commence from such positions as the working leg *pointe tendue* (as in *battements fondus*) when the teacher must insist that no weight remains over the working leg. There should even be a tiny shift of balance forwards if the working foot is raised from 5th position *derrière*, or backwards if raised from 5th *devant*. Once the weight is firmly established over the supporting leg the chain reaction begins as in *plié*. But it is not

75 Weight is centred through bones when supporting leg is straight.

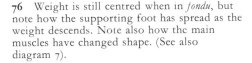

76 Weight is still centred when in *fondu*, but note how the supporting foot has spread as the weight descends. Note also how the main muscles have changed shape. (See also diagram 7).

quite the same. Children quickly discover how much easier it is to lift the working leg if the supporting one is in *fondu*. This happens firstly because the former carries no weight; and secondly the slight adjustment made in the central line of balance means that there has been a slightly changed relationship between the spine and the supporting leg. It now rests above the centre of one knee, and not between the centre of two legs (figures 75, 76 and diagram 7). Therefore some muscles emanating from or inserting below the inner side of the hip-joint work independently of those on the supporting side (in particular the sartorius and gracilis). But it is this freeing of muscles from weight on the working side that can disturb the line and balance of the dancer if those in the lumbar and sacral regions are not firmly controlled to hold the spine correctly over its centre (see also p. 46) and figures 85, 89, 92). The muscle most responsible is the psoas, which is also responsible for helping anyone to sit up and for raising the leg (see p. 86).

When first teaching *fondu* it is necessary to keep the working leg well extended from the hip-joint and controlled at the same level to which it is raised before *fondu* begins. The child will then feel how the pressure of the extra weight forces the supporting knee downwards as the muscles relax, and must not resist this pressure by tensing them round knee or ankle. He or she will then realise how much more strength is required throughout the supporting leg to push the weight of the body upwards again. Moreover he or she should also feel how much more effort is required to straighten the knee if there has been any slackening in all those muscles above the hip-joint which hold the spine erect and above its new centre. They will also discover how much more concentration is required to direct the supporting knee downwards whilst maintaining a correct turn-out without tensing. It is now, almost more than at any other time, that the true relationship between the talus, the bones of the leg and the arches of the foot must be maintained. The degree of turn-out in the hips should be carefully noted so that the supporting foot is placed at the same angle. The knee should then descend without any deviation from the line indicated, provided that there is strong muscular activity equally distributed within every part of the limb.

The easiest way for a child to feel the difference between carrying the weight over one or two feet is to perform a full *plié* in 1st position, then as the heels return to the floor when reaching *demi-plié*, lift one leg into low *retiré* and stretch the supporting leg upwards as the working knee is drawn still further upwards to the side (see also p. 46). The alteration made in the position of the balancing child should be very noticeable.

THE THREE BENDS OF THE ARMS

1. The fingers can bend downwards at any one of the three joints towards the palm of the hand except the thumb, which has only two joints. They can also stretch backwards a little.

2. The hand can bend forwards or backwards towards the lower arm at the wrist.

3. The lower arm can bend upwards from the elbow towards the shoulder or body at various angles. But like all other arm movements a stretching, raising or turning in one direction or another at wrist, elbow or shoulder level is required.

The most important *ports de bras* (carriage of the arms) is the maintenance of a rounded line at all times except when stretched into *arabesque*. But even this requires that same lift away from the body by using the muscles underneath the arms and shoulder-blades and NOT across the top and along the shoulders (see p. 22).

III. CHAIN REACTIONS IN SIMPLE PORTS DE BRAS

Commence with the arms hanging relaxed to the sides before bringing them into a state of tonicity. This shortens the muscles a little on the inside of the elbows, wrists and fingers. If the child is standing correctly the upper arms should be slightly stretched away from the body by the opening of the shoulder-blades and by the expansion of the rib-cage (see p. 21). Slightly stretch and group the fingers thus alerting the arm muscles so that they bring the middle fingers of each hand towards each other, feeling that the muscles beneath elbow and little finger are drawing the arms inwards without touching the body until they are *bras bas*. The fingers should be 2″–4″ (girls) and 4″–6″ (boys) apart, (see p. 101). If the relationship between the elbow and little finger is maintained at the same level, the child will understand how the middle bone of the hands will also retain its correct relationship with the centre line running through the bones of the arms. Too often hands are "sickled" outwards at the wrist.

The chain reaction starts when the upper arms are lifted slightly away from the body and the hands towards, but never crossing the centre line, and continues as the arms rise from *bras bas* to 1st position. The triceps (see diagram 5) lift the arms to the level of the breast-bone. The child should feel this lift gives more space to all those muscles encircling and/or connecting the rib-cage and spine with the shoulder-blades and arms, particularly the latissimus dorsi. These latter will be passively stretched as the child raises the arms from 1st to 5th position by using the triceps and biceps to lift their weight. But it is important when the outstretched and rounded, and therefore untensed, arms begin to rise above shoulder level on their way to 5th, that the upwards movement is countered by a strong downwards pull of the trapezius, which becomes active to keep the shoulder-blades still, helped by the outwards stretch of the deltoid to keep the arms rounded. This can only happen if the arms have been encouraged to move easily in the ball and socket joints of the shoulders.

Throughout the movement from 1st to 5th position it is worth suggesting that the arms must press against the forces of gravity. This helps a child to feel some resistance to the lifting upwards, particularly if the position and the relationship of the arms to each other in a rounded form is frozen – so to speak   during the ascent. A similar suggestion should be made during the descent to 1st position where the pressure is felt beneath the upper arm, particularly as the latissimus dorsi return to their normal length from shoulder to waist line and the deltoid and trapezius relax from their efforts of keeping the shoulders open.

When the arms descend from 5th to 2nd position the child should be encouraged to hold the arms in their rounded form as they part outwards as if the fingertips were tracing the outline of a circle just in front of their heads and bodies. The girl's circle will be a little further away than the boy's (see p. 101). But in neither case must elbows and wrists travel behind the shoulder line. Moreover if the circle is correctly shaped children will instinctively use that subtle turn of the arms in their sockets and bring the palms of the hands from their position facing the head, downwards to face front (see figures 7, 9). The fact that such a subtle change takes place in a major joint, linking limb to body, emphasizes the importance never to exaggerate the many varied movements which can take place in wrists and ankles. The former look fussy and the latter can be dangerous, and both distort the lines drawn by the whole limb.

1. The spine and head can bend forwards to several different degrees.
2. The spine and head can bend backwards to certain different levels.
3. The spine and head can bend to one side or the other.

All these bending or curving movements depend upon the degree of flexibility, capacity to stretch and the strength of the spinal muscles of each individual. They also depend upon that individual's sensitivity for "feeling" the amount of impetus to be given by the head when it directs the entire line of movement.

No classical dance movement requiring a bend or curve of the spine is desirable unless the dancer has firstly: stretched and straightened the spine as far as possible with turned-out legs (see p. 13), secondly: has slimmed the waist and taken the weight away from the legs (see pp. 13, 18), thirdly: freed the shoulders, arms and head from tension (see p. 22) and is capable of controlling the body throughout any movement involving the bending or curving of the spinal column in any direction.

It is of little value to discuss the bends of the head apart from those of the body. As will be seen below, the head does not necessarily play an active part in a body bend, but it always moves, if only passively because of its intimate relationship with the spine. However as it frequently plays a major part, the child must become aware of its importance in directing the line of movement early in training.

IV. CHAIN REACTIONS IN THE BODY. (i.e. *CAMBRÉ*)

It is essential to understand exactly which of these exercises (*cambré*) is being performed and when it is the body alone that moves and NOT the arms and shoulders.

Cambré 1. The Hinge-like Bend

Having taken correct stance at the barre, feet in 1st position (at the beginning it is best to work with feet not turned-out) breathe in and keeping the head and spine with arms in 2nd or 5th position, bend or "bow" straight forwards from the hip-joints which are the "hinge" upon which the movement depends. On no account should any muscle in the feet or legs relax, nor should the shoulder-blades strain backwards towards each other or relax inwards. The child should "feel" that the spine from coccyx to head is being pulled downwards in a straight line towards the floor and that all the vertebrae remain absolutely still and flat (photo 115 indicates that straight line required). As the muscles connecting and in front of the hip-joint and pelvis begin to relax, particularly those lying beneath the quadriceps, they are counter-balanced by the passive stretching downwards of the gluteus maximus and those terminating in the back of the knee (i.e. the hamstrings). Moreover the great spinal muscles stretch towards the head causing a passive stretching of the latissimus dorsi and trapezius so those across the abdomen relax very slightly. but not those controlling the lumbar and thoracic vertebrae which could disturb the relationship of the pelvis to the rib-cage. The calf muscles are also pulled upwards so that the strain on the Achilles tendon must be countered by a conscious "holding" at their normal length of all the peroneal, tibial and extensor muscles at the side and front of the ankles. This control continues downwards into the heels and through the foot to the toes, so that the talus is firmly held in its correct place.

The child should be encouraged to "bow" forwards as far as is comfortable because it is essential to keep the legs perpendicular to the floor and the spine straight. Those with sway-back legs, tight ham-strings and other physical problems will find this difficult. But provided there is sufficient pull upwards away from the waist, most children can "bow" to an angle of 120° to the floor, whilst those with normally straight legs soon manage to bow to 90°, their legs and bodies forming a right angle.

When returning to the upright position the same firm control must be exercised over the lumbar and lower thoracic muscles and particularly the recti abdominis, all of which must be strongly active in bringing the body upwards as the great spinal muscles and those connected with it return to their normal length. Too often the child attempts to pull the spine upwards by using the head and shoulders, thus curving the cervical and upper thoracic vertebrae backwards, a movement which occurs in *cambré 3* (p. 58), in which the head plays a part. It plays NO part in *cambré 1*.

Cambré 2. Curling Up and Down

This is in complete contrast to *cambré 1*. But is not, as many believe a complete relaxation of the body. It is a consciously practised movement to give greater flexibility to the spine. If there were complete relaxation, the child would fall. The curving starts from correct stance, feet in 1st position, arms hanging relaxed to the sides. The child then tries to curl the spine downwards throughout its length feeling that every vertebrae plays some part in the curving movement.

The head relaxes followed by the cervical vertebrae when the shoulders must be firmly controlled and kept freely opened sideways so that they neither relax nor strain backwards. As the muscles holding the twelve thoracic vertebrae in place are passively stretched at the back as the weight of the head descends, and by the increased curving of the spine forwards, some muscles in front of the rib-cage relax, but not the recti abdominis, which must keep the waist slimmed. The teacher should note carefully whether any stiffness appears between the 5th lumbar and 7th thoracic vertebrae, and as the head descends still further, bringing the lumbar vertebrae into the curve, whether any stiffness occurs in any part of the spine. A stiff or flat area anywhere between the 5th thoracic and 5th lumbar vertebrae can indicate how much flexibility might be expected if carefully trained. If the area is long in relationship to the length of the spine, or if it occurs between the 3rd lumbar and the 7th thoracic vertebrae efforts can be made to cultivate and make a little more flexible the muscles in this region. If the area is seen anywhere between the thoracic and cervical vertebrae this usually disappears with normal class-work. If however the child is unable to touch the toes or round the spine between the coccyx and 7th thoracic vertebrae, particularly between the coccyx and the 12th thoracic, it may be due to tight ham-strings, or tight Achilles tendons, or structural anomalies which require special attention to make all the muscles of the pelvic and thigh regions more responsive, and this is very difficult to achieve.

Cambré 3. The Gracious Bow as Used in Many Ports de Bras

When first teaching a child to bow as a thank-you gesture, it is sometimes best to eliminate the preparatory step to the side bringing the working leg, knee relaxed to *pointe tendue derrière*. Instead the *cambré* should be practised at the barre, standing correctly, feet in 1st and arms in 2nd position.

Begin to incline the body forwards in a straight line, but stretch the head and cervical spine upwards so that the head can, if required, move slowly round from one side to the other, the eyes focussing an imaginary audience. When the eyes have completed a half circle and the hinge-like bend is about a quarter of the way down, lower the head and slightly relaxing, bend forwards from the 5th thoracic vertebrae. This inclination of the body and head should be developed into the formal bow for boys, who do not usually bow so low as girls. The girls continue curving the body downwards without any further lowering of the head, to the 7th thoracic vertebrae and, if it is to develop into a deep *reverence*, as far as the waist. With both boy and girl the head and shoulders are held quite still at the level to which they bent when the eyes ceased to focus the imaginary audience. This requires more control than most children expect (figures 77–79).

Having descended as far as required, the head is then raised and must be "felt" to lead the body upwards to the erect position. It is the active participation of the head in this *cambré* that helps the child to understand the vital part it plays to direct the body through the correct line of movement as well as to be continually alert to the centering of weight. If it does not work correctly this *cambré* and the dancer will look lifeless and heavy. The very fact of having to keep the head and spine stretched upwards, whilst curving the spine forwards until that moment when eyes and head relax, helps to keep all the muscles of the spine in a state of tonicity, and teacher or audience recognise that the head has been bowed in an acknowledgement of thanks.

Cambré 4. For Use in Grands Ports de Bras

This is a combination of all the above *cambrés*, and should not be attempted until the student has firm control over the body. It is best practised firstly at the barre.

Standing correctly in 1st or 5th position with arms in 2nd, begin to lower the body as in *cambré 3*. At that point when the head should bow forwards, straighten the cervical vertebrae and stretch the spine outwards to continue downwards as in *cambré 1* until the body and legs form a right angle. Then, keeping all the muscles below the hip-joints firmly controlled so that the legs remain perpendicular to the floor, waist slimmed, relax the rest of the body and arms from above the hip-joints until the toes can be or are touched. Now bring the body upwards to the same point at which it relaxed and again stretch it straight outwards by strongly stretching all the spinal, buttock and abdominal muscles as well as those needed to bring the arm into 5th position. From the right angle now re-formed, pull the

58

The Spine During Reverence. Note the changes made in the spine, its muscles and the movement of the head. Note also that the working arm never over-crosses the centre in any of the following photographs.

77 *Pointe Tendue derrière.*

78 The body inclines, the head bends.

79 The body bends as the dancer steps back.

The Circling of the Body.

80   Bend sideways.

81   Curve forwards.

84   Lead the movement round the head.

85   Head leads the body round to the back.

82 Centre front bend.

83 Begin to curve sideways.

86 Centre back.

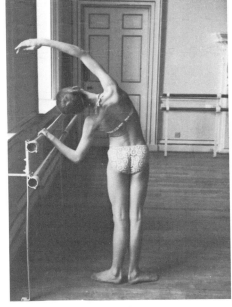

87 Returning to the side.

A Special Ports de Bras, Bending and Circling the Spine.

88 Arms 4th, feet 5th

89 Bend forwards and towards the front toe.

90 Change arms directly from 4th to 4th.

body straight upwards as in *cambré 1* until that moment when the head must take over so that the eyes again focus the audience, that is before the erect position is reached as in *cambré 3*. (This *cambré* can also begin with arms in 5th position).

Cambré 5. Stretching and Curving the Spine Backwards

No backwards bend should be attempted without first stretching the spine to its straightest, centering the weight firmly and freeing the head and shoulders from tension. It is also valuable slightly to incline and turn the head to one side or the other before the bend begins so that the child, particularly if short-sighted, is able to focus some line and keep control when beginning to curve backwards (see pp. 26, and 113).

The head begins to move and as the fully stretched cervical vertebrae relax and curl backwards so the sterno-mastoid and other muscles at the front of the neck and chest are passively stretched. At the same time the appropriate muscles control the shoulder-blades and arms (see p. 22) as in any forwards bend. An intake of breath is valuable in expanding the rib-cage and passively stretching the latissimus dorsi away from the spine as the muscles holding the vertebrae upright relax and shorten when the thoracic curve begins to increase.

91 Curve body round towards the back toe.   92 Recover position through sideways bend.

Except in specialised movements appropriate to would-be professionals, it is not advisable to allow children to curve the spine backwards below the waist-line. In fact if they are to remain standing in 1st or 5th positions with legs perpendicular it is rare that much curving takes place below the 7th thoracic vertebrae, although the muscles below this point stretch upwards to take part as they do in *arabesque* (see p. 19), because the muscles connected with the sacral, lumbar and lower thoracic vertebrae are passively but strongly pulled upwards by the equally strong stretching upwards of the recti abdominis as the weight of the body descends behind the spine without the child relaxing at the waist line.

A child with any stiffness in the above mentioned area will find a full back-bend difficult and will tend to arch the spine at the waist. This should be prevented because the contraction of muscles which would result means that the intervertebral discs between the 4th and 3rd, and the 2nd and 3rd lumbar vertebrae are pinched together and this can cause pain. In other cases such "arching" places too much strain on the sacro-iliac and hip-joints because the weight of the body is no longer carefully centred, particularly if the legs are fully turned-out.

It is better to encourage the child to bend the spine backwards only as far as is comfortable when first studying, and to gradually increase the curve as all the muscles between hip-joint and waist gain strength with the establishment of a firm turn-out. Back-bends are best practised in three stages. Firstly involve the head alone allowing no movement elsewhere (see p. 26); secondly stretch and curve the head and spine as far as the 5th thoracic vertebrae, which involves some stretching upwards of the recti abdominis, and a slight downwards pull of the muscle under the shoulder-blades; thirdly curve backwards as far as the 7th thoracic vertebrae which strongly influences all the muscles in buttocks and abdomen as well as those above the waist line.

Cambré 6. Sideways Bend

Sideways bend must also commence from correct stance, i.e. with feet in 1st or 5th position, and with an intake of breath and without allowing the waist to expand or the body to twist, try and lift the rib-cage a little further upwards before relaxing the latissimus dorsi and other muscles round and under the rib-cage on one side of the spine, whilst bending towards that side. The hips should be kept level, shoulders facing the same plane, but tilting towards the relaxed side, the head in the same relationship to the spine as when the bend commenced – i.e. the head DOES NOT MOVE.

Such a bend requires concentration and an understanding of how it is possible to divide those muscles which are attached to the spine and rib-cage so that those on one side can relax whilst those on the other stretch and gain length. This gives great freedom to certain movements when the centering of weight offers problems (e.g. *renversé en tournant en dehors*).

Cambré 7. Circling the Body

Once children can perform the above six *cambrés*, they should be encouraged to circle the body firstly as a small movement principally involving the upper half

64

from just below the shoulder-blades i.e. roughly at the level of the 5th thoracic vertebrae, and secondly from the waist. In all such movements the arms and shoulders play no part. All too frequently in such *cambrés* the arms are allowed to give impetus to the body by swinging in front or behind the shoulders which take part and throw the weight too far from the centre. But if the spine is to play its proper part, it must gain strength and independence to counter-balance the pull of the legs, arms and head. When practising any such circling movement it is often best to hold the arms in *demi-seconde* so that they are well away from the body and not too high. If they are held in 2nd, 5th or open 4th positions there can be too much stretching of those muscles connecting them with the shoulder joints, sometimes impeding the response of the latissimus dorsi, trapezius and deltoid to the need of relaxing when the body bends sideways and then circles at the same level forwards to the other side before curving backwards.

It is best to practise circling the body firstly at the barre, with feet in 1st or 5th positions and arm in *demi-seconde*. Breathe in and curve the body sideways towards the barre by relaxing the muscles under the shoulder-blades. Guide the body forwards and round to the other side by the head, gradually relaxing and then stretching the muscles in front and under the rib-cage. The weight of the head slightly bending forwards and preceding that of the upper part of the body also causes those muscles at the back to stretch and then relax as the vertebrae change relationships. These changes are very small in comparison with the total length of the spine, but those with any stiffness in the thoracic region will find the circling difficult, particularly if the child continues to circle the body round to the back and side again before recovering correct stance (see below).

As will be found later (see p. 80) any movement entailing a circling of the working leg from side to back, or back to side is difficult because of the adjustment to be made in the relationship between the raised leg and the body between the hip-joint and shoulder-blades. Similar difficulty is encountered when circling the body between side and back, and back and side. Yet this problem can be solved if the rib-cage is pulled upwards from the hip-joints and the legs pulled downwards thus keeping the waist slimmed, and allowing all the muscles above and below the central area to work unimpeded by wrongly placed weight. A dancer must always remember that the hip-joints and NOT the waist mark the dividing line of the body as a whole. The pelvis is so made and balanced above the legs, that like the talus, it must always be correctly centred to tilt forwards and upwards again, never backwards when the legs are turned-out. Thus having circled the body from side to front and side, the child must now consciously stretch the head straight outwards just as the body leaves the side and allow it to lead and circle the body round to the back and side again. Properly performed this will mean firstly that the cervical vertebrae are being activated to bring the body backwards and then continue by a parallel curving in the thoracic vertebrae just below the shoulder-blades. But there will be no relaxation in the deep muscles between rib-cage and hip-joints. These remain firmly controlled throughout.

At a later stage in training this circling can be done at a lower level provided that the spine is given freedom to move correctly with the proper co-ordination

65

of arms, shoulder-blades and legs. It is best performed from 5th position, arms in open 4th, opposite arm raised to foot in front, the arm and shoulder being held still, the head leading the bending and circling of the spine, the hand only playing a tiny part by a turn of the wrist to bring the palm into its correct relationship with the head and arms (figures 80–87).

From time to time teachers and choreographers require students to acquire even greater flexibility by allowing the body between the hip-joints and waist to take part in some *grands ports de bras*. In such exercises it should be clearly understood whether the arms are to play a major part or not in the total movement. The following is an example of how both body and arms can take part, or merely the arms accompanied by a simple forwards bend and straightening of the body. It is best practised from 5th position *croisé*, arms in open 4th, opposite arm raised to foot in front. Breathe in, turn the body and bend forwards as far as possible towards the front toe. The turn should come from the waist, legs firmly controlled and hips level. At the lowest point change the arms directly from 4th to 4th position as the body circles round until the newly raised arm is at least over, if not beyond the back toe. Stretch upwards changing the arms through 1st as the body returns to be correctly centred as at the beginning. At no point in the circling must either arm go behind its own shoulder (figures 88–92).

If this exercise is practised alternately with the same movements of the arms but the body bending only straight forwards and stretching directly upwards, the arms changing at the lowest point, even a child begins to understand the effect made by a slight change in the use of the body. A change that is nowhere more important than in *grands ronds de jambe en l'air* (see p. 80) or *renversé en tournant en dehors* where the dancer all but over-balances as he or she circles the working leg from the side to *arabesque* and *attitude*, before curving the body sideways away from the supporting leg on beginning to turn backwards, then on continuing the turn, has to relax and circle the body downwards, forwards and immediately upwards to complete the *pas de bourrée* fully erect and calm in 5th position.

V. CHAIN REACTIONS WHEN STRETCHING AND RAISING THE LEG

Although the above paragraphs stress the passive stretching of certain muscles when others relax and the weight of the body descends into a *plié* or *fondu*, some emphasis has been made upon those same muscles when they must become active to restore the weight correctly over two or one leg during the ascent. The next movements to study are those entailing an active stretching of the muscles in one straight leg when relieved from weight prior to being raised to some height at the front, side or back. These involve every muscle in the working leg to a greater or lesser degree, whilst those on the supporting side remain still and firmly controlled with the turn-out maintained, hips at the same level and spine erect. It is now essential that, as the working leg begins to move, the weight is transferred correctly and centred over the supporting leg. Although this transfer is scarcely visible, particularly when moving from 5th position, it must be done to free all muscles connecting pelvis, femur and knee, particularly those on the inside of the leg. It should be remembered that the muscles of the legs are not quite in the same relationship as they were when in correct stance. (As the legs are now turned-out the term "inside" indicates all the muscles and ligaments behind the knee and ankle and "outside" those in front.) The muscles of the supporting femur and lower leg may be said to run in straighter, slightly shorter lines between the pelvis and knee because of the pressure and slight movement of the body to centre the weight over the bones, whilst those on the working side can now be moved in diagonal (horizontal, and above when lifted) and thus longer lines. Therefore it is the biceps, gluteus maximus, gracilis and adductors, countered by the sartorius stretching from the outside to inside of both legs, which must be re-educated to work at their maximum length.

1. Battements Tendus

A chain reaction begins as the working leg is freed from weight and the heel, moving from 1st or 5th position, presses outwards along the floor away from the supporting leg. The muscles on the inside from crutch to knee and ankle actively stretch down to keep the heel on the floor as long as possible, whilst those on the outside under the quadriceps, and the quadriceps themselves remain at their normal length to keep the leg straight. However as soon as the heel leaves the floor pulled upwards by the action of the muscles terminating in the Achilles tendon and extending behind the heel, those in front of the leg emanating from the knee and continuing into the foot react and stretch further downwards until the tips of the toes rest on the floor, the muscles under the instep having been fully tightened. This final stretching downwards should also passively stretch the quadriceps a little because of their links with the lower leg and because they too must work at their maximum length if the dancer is to benefit from a fully stretched working leg when it has to be raised from the floor. Moreover a full stretch downwards from the hip-joint facilitates its work as a hinge both when the leg moves upwards or the body moves downwards.

This stretching of the inside leg muscles must be accompanied by a strong control and drawing together of all those keeping the spine erect in the region between the coccyx and waist. But the muscles in the buttocks must not be "clenched" and need not be if the recti abdominis are fully stretched upwards to give room for the muscles rising from knee to pelvis. *Battements tendus* to front and side should be easier to perform once this greater extension away from the hip socket had been mastered because the central line of the working leg from hip-joint to toes can be held as it moves outwards. However there are two difficult moments; firstly when the heel, and secondly when the metatarsal arch leaves the floor. At each moment the child must stretch equally all those muscles in front of the ankle and secondly tighten all those under the instep so that there is no "sickling in or out", which can result if the foot is not stretched directly downwards because the child has forgotten that the foot slopes a little backwards from the big to the little toe joint (see p. 34 and figures 93–100).

This centre line must also be held as the foot glides back to 1st or 5th position,

93 The unturned but stretched leg in *pointe tendue devant*.

94 The leg has been fully turned-out from the hips. Note the lines of the muscles pulling downwards to the toes as well as upwards to the hip-joint.

95 The leg is raised fully stretched.

68

the foot gradually descending to the floor through the metatarsal arch, instep and heel. The easiest way for a child to understand the difficulty of centering the line of the straight leg is to ensure that the foot bends directly upwards and downwards at the ankle without deviating to one side or another. This is particularly important when moving to the back when an attempt should be made to raise the body even further from the hip-joints of both supporting and working legs. This lift allows a little more freedom to stretch the working leg further outwards without losing turn-out and prevents the child twisting the pelvis. It is particularly difficult for those with sway-back legs. But by raising the body further upwards, they can bring the weight a little further forwards and thus feel the passive stretching of the quadriceps and not an active one in the ham-strings which pulls the knee backwards.

2. Battements Glissés and Jetés

The action of pressing the whole foot outwards along the floor in *battements tendus* is all important when the leg has to be raised into *battements glissés* and higher. The slight friction created by the pressure causes the muscles under the instep and toes to spread a little so that the nerves in the sole of the foot react sensitively as they "feel" this friction and immediately contract to give impetus and lift the foot upwards when the toes lose contact with the floor. This vital impetus must be cultivated until the child realises how little or how much pressure and strength in the muscles of ankle, instep and metatarsal arch are required to raise the leg to different heights.

The speed at which the final tightening of the muscles under the instep is accomplished determines any height below 30°. This does not mean that the movement need be slow or fast. On the contrary the slower the movement outwards and the greater the pressure, the greater the friction and nerve reaction, and thus a greater impetus to lift the leg. But for an ordinary *battement glissé* a steady pressure should be enough.

If the leg has to be lifted above 30°, as in *battements jetés* to any height up to 45° (those with strong muscles will lift to 60°), there must be enough pressure to set up a stronger reaction. This requires a quicker stretching of the instep as the metatarsal arch leaves the floor so that the impetus already given by the friction can be "felt" higher up the leg and set up some reaction in the biceps and gluteus maximus to lift the leg. This and the stretch of those on the inside of the leg crossing and continuing down below the knees to the toes gives greater length and ultimately height because the lengthening is countered by those which help to lift the leg. It can then be held at this new height because no further muscular activity is required, the leg has been freed from weight, the toes are pointed and the muscles are held at the appropriate lengths. However the teacher should ensure that the child carries the weight of the body further forwards and stretched upwards when the *battements jetés* are performed to the back. As in *battements glissés*, children, particularly those with sway-back legs, must "tilt" the pelvis forwards when lifting the leg above 30°. By so doing they will learn to pull up the

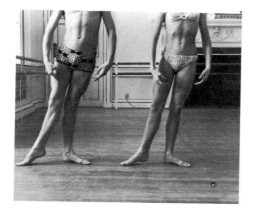

96 The heel has just left the floor.

97 The foot then rises on to the metatarsal arch.

98 The foot is fully stretched. Note difference in muscular development between boy and girl.

99 Both legs are fully stretched and the working leg extended outwards from the hip-joint.

100 Judith has not stretched her leg away from the hip-joint, therefore her supporting hip is out of line and the shoulders are tensed.

70

rectus femoris (see p. 14) and keep the knee straight, this centering of the lines of both legs should ensure the supporting leg remains perpendicular to the floor.

3. Grands Battements

Because *grands battements* require a greater impetus from the working leg, it is useful to decide which type of movement is needed when lifting the leg to 90° and over. The Russian *battements relevés* demand a slow and completely controlled raising of the leg from a closed position to 90° at least, whilst *grands battements* common to most schools require a "throwing" of the leg to the highest point where it can be held – if the dancer is strong enough – or lowered as quickly as it ascends. Both forms are extremely valuable. The former gives strength and control and the latter helps to loosen the limbs and is a vital part of many steps of elevation (i.e. *grand jeté en tournant*). But in both the dancer has to determine the amount of impetus and where it should originate. Moreover in both types the dancer must clearly understand that the working leg alone performs. In no case must the spine take part. This will occur if there is any weakening or "tucking in" by the muscles holding the pelvis and hips in place (figures 101–107).

Battements relevés commence from 5th position, with arms in 2nd. Slowly stretch the leg outwards with firm pressure until it is fully extended to *pointe tendue devant* and without pausing continue to "feel" how the leg is still being stretched outwards away from the hip-joint. But as the toe leaves the floor "feel" it is also being lifted from underneath by the biceps and gluteus maximus and a slight tightening of the quadriceps. So far the movement is very like a slow *battement jeté* to 45°. But when the leg rises above 45°, the quadriceps tighten still further as the ham-strings are passively lengthened and both are kept in straight lines by the action of the gracilis and sartorius countering each other to maintain turn-out. At this point the psoas, a very powerful but invisible muscle, rising in front of the lumbar vertebrae, passing down through the groin and attached to the inner side of the femur, comes into play. So far it has helped to keep the pelvis in its correct relationship to the classically straightened spine. But now it contracts with the tightening of the quadriceps and helps the gluteus maximus and other muscles to raise the leg to 90°, provided the ham-strings have not lost length by tension. Because the psoas is intimately connected to the spine, hip-joint and femur it gives impetus to the recti abdominis and muscles within the diaphragm to react. They now stretch upwards still further to counter-balance the action of the quadriceps and psoas in order to free the hip-joint for its work as a pivot or "hinge" (figures 103, 104).

Battement relevé to the side is more difficult to perform because the pelvic bone structure and Y-shaped and pubo-femoral ligaments do not allow the leg to rise much higher than 45°, although the dancer may have a well turned-out flexible leg. As soon as a height is reached when the pelvis will "tilt" upwards on the side if the leg rises higher, the ham-strings and biceps must be lengthened further where the muscles insert behind the hip-joint as the gluteus maximus and psoas help to raise the weight further upwards. If the dancer concentrates on trying to hold the hips level as this lift takes place by consciously "feeling" all those muscles which

71

Grand Battement Devant.

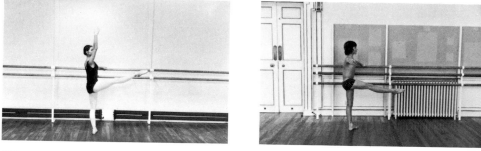

101   102

Devant with erect spine, head alert, hips level, working leg stretched away from the body. Note lift away from the waist in both boy and girl.

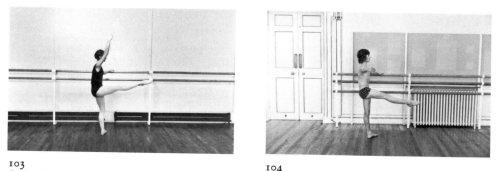

103   104

Carina has "tucked in her tail" so has used her spine and not the leg muscles to raise her legs. Stephen has placed his weight too far back.

hold the spine and weight of the body steady over the supporting leg, it will be found that the hip-level hardly changes at all. The muscles of the working leg have not only worked independently of those on the supporting side, but have been lengthened away from the hip-joints and under the leg, because those on the outside contract and shorten (i.e. the quadriceps). This only happens if the central lines of both legs have not been twisted.

Battements relevés derrière are the most difficult to perform. They commence when the dancer slowly reaches the same height as in *battements glissés* at 30° (see p. 69). At this moment the pelvis "tilts" forwards. But as the leg moves upwards the dancer should "feel" that although the head is drawing the spine outwards and into a "bow", this inclination must be countered and the head, followed by the cervical and upper seven thoracic vertebrae must be stretched and curved backwards towards the centre of an *arabesque* lying directly over the perpendicular supporting leg. As the upper half of the body stretches upwards and backwards the dancer raises the leg a little faster. In so doing he or she must remember not to shorten the waist between the hip-joints and lower ribs as well as to retain exactly at the same level the latissimus dorsi and trapezius on both sides of the spine

72

Grand Battement Side.

105 *À la seconde*. The head is correctly centred over an erect spine, leg and instep. The shoulders are level and the working leg stretched away from the body.

106 The result of sinking on the supporting side.

107 The result of "tucking in" the working leg at the hip joint.

The Arabesque.

108   A well-stretched *arabesque.*

109   Muscles under shoulder-blades to waist have not been stretched on the working side.

---

between the various vertebrae, shoulder-blades and arms. This requires stretching the quadriceps and other muscles on the outside of the working leg countered by a contraction of the gluteus maximus and if possible, a further stretching of the ham-strings on the inside of the working leg. In this way a curved line from head to toe can be "felt" to be equally balanced and centred between the coccyx and waist. It is not an angle made at the waist by arching the back. This latter is caused by failing to slim the waist, lifting the leg higher by tensing the ham-strings, clenching the buttock muscles and straining the shoulder-blades backwards. It can be dangerous (figures 108–111).

Grands Battements to the front and side require the strongest possible impetus from the pressure of the foot along the floor, which carries the leg straight up-wards towards the centre of an *arabesque* lying directly over the perpendicular leg by the strong pressure and swift reaction of the muscles in the sole of the foot should be such that the leg is "thrown" into the air by a simultaneous lift from the gluteus maximus and the muscles below and a contraction of the quadriceps and psoas and, as the toes leave the floor, a lengthening of the ham-strings. The instep remains stretched. This "throw" also needs a further stretch upwards of the recti abdominis and a contraction of the muscles controlling the Y-shaped and pubo-femoral ligaments. But the "throw" must not be so powerful that the child cannot control the perpendicular supporting leg. Once again it should be stressed that all muscles holding the weight over its proper centre should be firmly controlled (figures 101–107).

Grands Battements derrière require the same impetus as to the side and front. But as the toe leaves the floor there should be a simultaneous lift from the gluteus maximus and biceps and a lengthening of the ham-strings, gracilis and sartorius from hip-joint to below the knee as the spine stretches upwards and backwards

110 Hips have not been kept facing the same plane and shoulders are rounded.

111 Carina has "arched" her back in an effort to keep her spine erect.

with the "tilt" of the pelvis. However this "throw" must not affect the supporting leg nor twist the body out of alignment. The *arabesque* should be clearly visible and if necessary held when the leg is at its height (figures 108–111).

When performing *grands battements devant* the dancer can begin to study the most difficult transfer of weight which takes place in the air, e.g. *grande jeté en avant*. The *grands battements devant* described above are performed with the spine and head fully erect and the impetus given by the working leg should be such that if it were reinforced by a *fondu* and simultaneous spring from the supporting leg, the dancer would be propelled straight upwards as in a *grand fouetté sauté* (figure 121). Thus both legs are responsible to carry the dancer into the direction indicated by the head. At the height of the jump he or she can then turn into *arabesque* and descend into *fondu* on the same leg and at the same spot where the jump began.

If however a *grand jeté en avant* is required, the *grands battements* should be practised from 5th position, same arm raised as working leg, with the head and body stretched and curved slightly backwards. This backwards inclination of the body should be sufficient to reinforce the impetus given by both the supporting and working legs as the former springs into the air simultaneously with the "throw" of the latter. The weight of the body being slightly behind the direction of the jump, then propels the dancer upwards along and down in a curving line so that as the front leg descends, an *arabesque* has been formed, and can be held as the new supporting leg descends into *fondu* before stretching upwards into the pose already created.

It is well to note that John Weaver included jumping when discussing to rise or raise, and closely connected this with the anticipating of direction by the head, mentioning its importance in most movements where the body travels through space. These ideas upon the powerful impetus that can be given by the correct

75

movement and positioning of the head were no doubt in Noverre's mind when he added to glide and dart to Weaver's original four movements.

John Weaver also makes it clear that to raise (rise) in dancing can also mean to stretch. It has been noted that an essential feature of battement *relevé* to front and side is the "feeling" that the leg is stretched outwards at the same time it is being raised (see p. 66). It is useful to understand how this happens by analysing some simple movements where one and then another part of the working leg moves independently to give impetus before describing *développés* in which all three movements are needed and in which every muscle plays a part.

4. Retirés, Coupés and Petits Jetés

A simple *retiré* has already been mentioned (see p. 40). If it is small all that is needed is a relaxation of the muscles behind the knee, a stretch and/or contraction of those below to point the foot and a raising of the bent leg by the biceps etc. (see p. 66). Whether the leg moves from 1st or 5th position a transfer of weight to the supporting leg takes place. But the track made by the rising leg is all important if balance is to be maintained whenever a *retiré* is used, either as a preparation or as an end in itself.

If the *retiré* commences in 1st, the foot should be drawn backwards to the supporting heel as the knee bends and the instep stretches. The transfer is completed as the toe leaves the floor and is drawn up the side of the leg to the requisite height. If however the *retiré* begins from 5th, the working leg should be raised in such a way that by the time the instep is fully stretched the toe leaves the floor in front or behind the CENTRE of the supporting foot, the weight now being transferred (see p. 40). It is then drawn up diagonally TO THE SIDE of the supporting knee if some stretching movement is to follow (e.g. *développé* see p. 78 and figure 112). If on the other hand a *retiré passé* is required, the toe traces another slightly diagonal line down the opposite side of the supporting leg until the toe reaches the end of the calf, whereupon the ankle followed by the heel arrives in a correct 5th position without any shifting of either foot.

In both *retiré simple* and *passé* the child should realise the exact centre line of both legs as well as the degree of turn-out needed so that the working foot does not "sickle in or out" by wrapping round the calf because it has been overcrossed, or not kept in proper relationship to the supporting leg. The ankle bone marks the centre over which the weight is balanced, therefore the pointed toe should trace a line from that centre to the side of the supporting knee when moving from 5th whether the relationship of the feet should change or not at the end of the movement.

Keeping this extremely close relationship of legs and feet is of vital importance in such quick transfers of weight as a preparatory *coupé* before a *chassé* or *assemblé*, or even *petits jetés*, for although the action of the latter is not quite the same, the relationship between the two legs as the weight is swiftly transferred from one to the other must be as intimate as in a simple *coupé*. Thus the working foot is pressed upwards and away from the centre as the *jeté* begins and returns to that centre as it descends to take the weight and replace the erstwhile supporting leg. This has also risen beneath the centre and is free to be pressed outwards in its turn.

5. *Petits Battements sur le Cou-de-pied*

Children find it difficult to perform *petits battements sur le cou-de-pied*. They may not be able to hold the working leg in position and allow the lower leg to move independently by relaxing the muscles under the knee and control those in the hip-joint so that the lower half of the leg and particularly the tips of the toes trace an acute angle on the floor. They should move outwards and inwards from the front to the back of the supporting ankle and vice-versa.

First stretch the working foot *pointe tendue* then bend the foot upwards at the ankle keeping the instep stretched. Raise the knee bringing the foot inwards until the centre below the instep rests above the ankle of the supporting foot. Stretch the instep down again until the tips of the toes touch the floor. As in *retiré* the centres of the legs have been drawn together again, ankle resting above ankle. From this position, and if the muscles under the knee are sufficiently relaxed, the child should be able to trace the angle required without any pressure being placed on the toes. Admittedly this needs much thought because so few muscles motivate this tiny movement and are so closely linked with others whose concern is to prevent anything but the lower leg moving in one piece from the knee downwards.

There are other positions used for *petits battements*. That in which the working foot is wrapped round just above the supporting ankle can be dangerous for all but experienced dancers as it results in a "sickled foot" and poor landing after some beaten step. Or the foot can be fully stretched, the tips of the toes moving to and fro just above the level of the supporting ankle or below the calf. These are useful when practising how to descend on one foot after an *entrechat trois* etc. But in such examples the movement still comes only from the knee downwards.

This relaxation is not used for some *petits battement battus* or *serrés* where the fully pointed foot is beaten just in front or behind the instep of the supporting foot on full or *demi-pointe*, the toes just missing the floor. When used as a preparation for *cabriole devant* or *derrière* the beat should originate in the hip-joint, the entire working leg being moved outwards and inwards by the action of all the muscles in and round that hip-joint, the knee only being very slightly bent so that when the proper step is performed, both legs can be seen to be fully stretched.

6. *Battements Frappés and Fondus*

The movements mentioned in section 5 should help a child to understand how some part of a leg can move independently of another. *Petits battements battus* or *serrés* require no impetus nor do they give impetus. But they can and should be accented if they are to serve their proper purpose as preparations to such steps as the quick snatch upwards into a *retiré* for a *pirouette*; or to mark the amount of beats or crossing of the legs to perform in *batterie*. *Battements frappés* and *fondus* (also *fouettés*) however both give and require impetus, particularly if correctly accented to lead the dancer into the next movement.

77

The impetus given by any *battement frappé* comes from the knee and should be strong enough to carry the dancer into a jump towards some point if there has also been a preparatory *fondu* then a simultaneous spring from the supporting leg as the working one is strongly brushed outwards for *sur le cou-de-pied*. This position is not identical with that used for *petits battements* (see p. 77). The foot must be so placed that when the leg is stretched, the toes push into the floor at such an angle that the area between the metatarsal arch and tips have enough friction and impetus to cause a reaction in the muscles under the knee to raise and stretch the leg. The amount of impetus will largely depend upon the angle and speed at which the knee straightens and the foot stretches outwards. It also depends upon the amount of controlled strength the child places into the movement from the knee – which must NOT be jerked. If it is suggested that the accent is strongly emphasized AWAY from the body and held when the leg is fully extended he or she should be able to "feel" the outwards accent needed to travel to a new centre.

An alteration in the timing of the above with an accent INWARDS will introduce the child to that particular type of "whipping" (*fouetté*) movement required for a *flic-flac*, where the impetus given by the foot and knee starting from a *fondu* and simultaneous rise to *demi-pointes* on the supporting leg should be sufficient to turn the child at least half the way round. A similar even stronger "whipping" movement is required when the working leg passes through 1st position as a preparation for *grand fouetté en tournant*.

Battements fondus could be described as movements teaching how to control and sustain a series of poses in which both legs must be synchronised to relax and stretch continuously so that the body sinks and rises smoothly and effortlessly. From *pointe tendue* (see p. 67) both legs simultaneously relax, the one into *retiré*, only the lower half bending until the toe reaches the bottom of the calf of the other, which relaxes into *fondu*. The amount of bend should be equal in both legs. To return both legs to their proper length requires the strength of the supporting leg to push the weight of the body upwards from the *fondu* (see p. 51) and as the working leg is already at the requisite height, only enough to stretch the muscles behind the knee and open the lower leg. If the child is encouraged to "feel" an accent both INWARDS and DOWNWARDS towards and over the supporting foot, he or she should also be able to "feel" the strength needed to push the weight UPWARDS and the leg OUTWARDS without over-balancing because the working leg has been incorrectly controlled and timed. Moreover if required to rise still further to *demi-pointes*, he or she will realise that control over the height and speed of the unfolding is all important. The full stretch should not be reached until the weight of the body is firmly centred over the much smaller area. It should be insisted that the supporting heel is firmly on the floor with knee straight before the rise to *demi-pointes* (see p. 35 and figures 75, 76).

7. Développés

Grands développés to front, side and back require more control, strength and carefully directed impetus than any other movement. By the time these are added to the vocabulary the child has learnt to bend, stretch and raise the leg in various types of movement. He or she can still use these same techniques and achieve a fairly satisfactory *développé*. But it will not have that sweep of line which can be managed if greater attention is paid to an important detail.

The moment when this important detail must be brought into use is immediately after the working leg has been raised into *retiré*. The weight must be accurately centred with the raising of the pointed toe at least as far as the centre of the turned-out supporting knee. From thence it can be stretched outwards to front and side, or with a forwards "tilt" of the pelvis to the back. But in most cases no matter how hard the child tries, as the leg is slowly stretched the line of the leg will lower. If however the bent leg is raised a little higher with a simultaneous slight opening of the knee, this will release muscles between the pelvis and behind and under the knee which have been contracted during the *retiré*. This slight lifting and opening allows the biceps, gluteus maximus and those muscles lying beneath more freedom to keep the leg raised and be stretched outwards as the hamstrings are extended. Similarly when *développé derrière* is performed, as the bent leg leaves *retiré*, the knee can be carried round to *attitude* together with the slight "tilt" forwards of the pelvis and a raising of the lower leg (see figure 116). This circling allows the dancer to maintain turn-out because the quadriceps and muscles under the gluteus maximus can maintain their new classical relationship. But once the lower leg stretches backwards and the pelvis "tilts" forwards with the specialised curving of the spine into *arabesque*, the quadriceps and gluteus maximus can be said to change functions as in *battements relevés* (i.e. the former must be stretched and the latter contracted to hold the leg in place see p. 71). This tiny movement of opening, raising and slightly rotating the bent leg in the hip-joint introduces a child to the extra effort needed to slim the waist as much as possible whenever the working leg has to move from side to back and vice-versa at any height above 45°. To practise the slight rotation with the leg bent at a fairly open angle makes it easier because the leg is shorter and lighter to move, and the many muscles which counter-balance each other when the leg is stretched, are held passive and play no part in the rotation. Only those ordering the rotation and holding the raised leg have to work, i.e. the gluteus maximus and muscles lying beneath and the psoas. The rest only start work when the bent leg stretches outwards from *attitude to arabesque* (see figures 117, 118 and 136, 137).

VII. CHAIN REACTIONS WHEN STRETCHING, ROTATING OR CIRCLING THE LEGS

The action of turning the leg outwards to achieve classical stance gives the child some idea of the chain reaction set in motion when the leg has to circle *à terre* or *en l'air*, throughout the various types of *ronds de jambe* the same control for turn-out must be exercised over exactly the same muscles to keep the spine erect and still, the weight firmly centred over the supporting leg and the working one fully extended from the hip socket. It is needed to give the leg and buttock muscles as much freedom as possible to rotate gently in the socket at the awkward moments when the pelvis either "tilts" forwards when the leg passes from side to back, or recovers its upright position when the leg passes from back to side (figures 112–119).

8. Ronds de Jambe à terre

The chain reaction of any *rond à terre* begins as it does in any *battement tendu* and before the circling begins. The working leg must be extended fully to *pointe tendue devant* (or *derrière*) and the move from front to side is comparatively easy if no muscle is tensed and no attempt made to change the relationship of the leg and pelvis. If the toe is used as the point of a pencil in compasses and the curve made correctly centred through the leg to the middle toe, the child can feel, if a hand is placed on the gluteus maximus or the quadriceps that as the former shortens a little to bring the leg from front to side, the latter will lengthen to give proper shape to the circle. Moreover the gracilis and sartorius, countering each other to hold turn-out will also help other muscles to adjust the leg to its new position; i.e. the knee and foot no longer face outwards and sideways (as in front) but the ceiling. As the leg moves from side to back these same muscles continue to act, re-adjusting the leg to its new position at the back as the gluteus maximus contracts and the quadriceps lengthen. A *rond en dedans* merely reverses the action of the same muscles if care is taken to feel that the buttock of the working leg is being drawn downwards and towards the coccyx as it moves from back to side and then front. But it cannot circle forwards or backwards if the weight has been allowed to sink either on to the supporting or working hip, or if the pelvis has been twisted by over-emphasis of the turn-out at the side.

The completion of each *rond* in a series requires detailed attention. The working foot must return to 1st position in exactly the same way as it does during the close of a *battement tendu*. It must sink through toes, metatarsal arch and instep until the heel is once again firmly pressed on to the floor at right angles to its own leg and besides the supporting heel as it passes through 1st and stretches directly forwards or backwards to commence another *rond* AFTER reaching *pointe tendue*.

9. Ronds de Jambe en l'Air (figures 112–119)

These can be taken from *battement relevé* or *développé* at any height. As mentioned earlier (p. 71) as soon as the leg rises beyond 45° (side) or 30° (back) awkward moments will occur if the child does not remember to "tilt" the pelvis. The moment when this occurs varies a little with the individual and depends upon the shape and size of the hips, the amount of turn-out and the dancer's ability to keep the body fully extended between hip-joint and shoulder-blades on both sides of the spine.

The chain reaction for a *rond de jambe en l'air en dehors* begins after the leg has been raised or stretched to any height (usually above 45°) and resembles that of a *ronde à terre*. But because the gluteus maximus, biceps, psoas and quadriceps have greater responsibility to hold the leg at the appropriate height, more care should be taken to keep the weight centred, the spine erect and pelvis still during the first quarter circle. Perhaps more important is to ensure that the working arm, when at the barre (or both when in the centre) is held and moved correctly without tension so that the latissimus dorsi and trapezius are stretched diagonally outwards

Grand Rond de Jambe En Dehors.

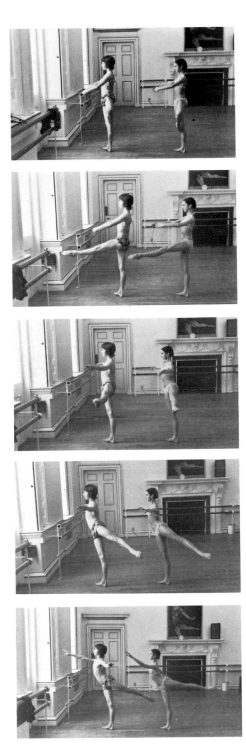

112 *Retiré,* spines erect, weight well centred.

113 *Developpé* devant. Weight remains centred spines erect.

114 To the side, arms open to stabilise balance, bodies remain as before.

115 The leg is half-way between side and back, pelvis is beginning to tilt and the waist is more slimmed.

116 *Arabesque.* Both have tilted forwards from the pelvis and curved their spines and heads backwards to centre their weight.

Grand Rond de Jambe En Dedans.

117 Front view of working leg leaving *retiré* to show stretch of working leg outwards in *developpé*. Both boy and girl have unfortunately raised the working hip.

118 The *arabesque* from the above *retiré*.

119 The awkward moment when the leg is returning to side and the spine and pelvis must once more be stretched upwards.

away from the spinal column to keep the shoulder open (see p. 18), then the recti abdominis and other muscles will keep the waist slimmed and rib-cage firm. Simultaneously with the leg leaving the side to circle to the *arabesque* and with an intake of breath, the pelvis must "tilt" forwards from the hinge, and the cervical vertebrae and head stretch and curve backwards (see p. 19). The amount of "tilt" will depend upon the height of the raised leg. The dancer should feel that the same counter-balancing of effort between the gluteus maximus and quadriceps and the holding of the turn-out by the sartorius and gracilis as is felt when circling *à terre*. But extra length is needed both at the front and back of the knee if the leg is to be fully stretched. The dancer should feel that the leg is being pulled even further backwards from both the front and back of the pelvis and hip-joint as the appropriate muscles, emanating from the same area also pull upwards and outwards towards the head. In this way the hips can be kept practically level and facing the same plane. As the late Seraphina Astafieva used to say: "In *Arabesque* pull yourself in half so that there is a true centre between your head and toe, and it is over your support" (see figures 113–116).

Rond de jambe en l'air en dedans is always more difficult to perform, partly because the dancer often forgets to stretch the recti abdominis when raising or stretching the leg at the back and neglects to free shoulders, head and arms from tension as the pelvis "tilts" forwards. If however tension is absent as the leg begins its circle to the side, the same technique applies as it does *à terre*. But the body must move

Arabesque Allongé.
120 Judith's body is nearly at a right angle to her supporting leg as she tries to stretch into a straight line.

simultaneously upwards with the leg movement so that it is fully erect when the working leg reaches side. Again it should be stressed that if the waist is kept slimmed and the buttock muscles in the working leg felt to be drawn inwards towards the coccyx, this difficult change in relationship of the leg to the hip-joint can be smoothly accomplished. The action of drawing the buttock downwards releases the gluteus maximus, which causes the quadriceps to contract and hold the leg in place (figures 117–119).

The equal balancing of the body between head and toe mentioned above is very important in advanced work when the dancer has to flatten the body in *allongé* (figure 120) so that a straight line runs between them. But it is not difficult if the dancer has the courage to "tilt" straight from the "hinge" as in *cambré* 1 (see p. 56), at the same time as the leg is stretched or raised at the back. However it is vital that the weight is correctly centred whether the supporting leg is straight or *fondu*, and the dancer feels the strong pull outwards of the leg muscles away from the hip-joint and pelvis. He or she should also feel a straight horizontal line in the same way as a perpendicular line when balancing on one leg. It is only achieved if there is a full understanding of how the four curves of the spine can be straightened and stretched to the best advantage (figures 138, 139, 140).

The same forwards "tilt" of the pelvis from the hinge over a perpendicular supporting leg is needed in *penché* (figure 135). But the body does not "tilt" into a straight line. Usually an *arabesque* is performed before *penché* and must be held as the body moves downwards and the working leg upwards. If the head is tensed during this descent the movement will be inhibited. But if it is allowed slowly and slightly to incline forwards, leading the body downwards it helps the dancer to straighten the cervical and upper thoracic vertebrae. This slight straightening of the spine better balances the lifting of the leg because too curved a line in *penché* throws the weight backwards towards the supporting leg, which moves out of the perpendicular, to counteract which the dancer arches the spine, spoiling both line and balance.

10. Rotation and Grands Fouettés

Both rotation and *grands fouettés* (*relevés* or *sautés*) set up a similar reaction to that of *grand rond de jambe en l'air*, but should not be practised until the dancer has mastered the art of "tilting" and/or restoring the pelvis to its correct position as the working leg circles from side to back or vice-versa-. It also requires the ability to rise and make a quarter or half turn on *demi-* or full *pointe* (or during a jump) on the supporting leg, because both legs rotate simultaneously and slightly in the hip-sockets to bring the dancer round to the new position.

When performed at the barre the chain reaction begins as the leg is raised or stretched forwards above 45° and held fully extended as in *battement relevé* (see. p. 71). From thence the movement should be practised in two stages so that when the movement is temporarily halted half-way round, the dancer can ensure that the legs are in correct relationship; i.e. from a preparatory *fondu*, breathe in and rise to *demi-pointe* making a quarter turn so that the dancer is *à la seconde* with spine erect, waist slimmed, hips level and raised leg held. This requires a slight rotation of both legs, the supporting one outwards and the raised one inwards. This can be accomplished if, at the moment of *fondu*, the muscles on the insides of both legs relax a little before stretching with the rise to *demi-pointes*. The rotation continues with another *fondu* and rise to *demi-pointes* making another quarter turn during which the pelvis must "tilt" forwards as the gluteus maximus, quadriceps and other muscles in the raised leg are again slightly rotated inwards to bring the dancer into *arabesque*. It is this second stage which is difficult. But the dancer should remember that it is the entire pelvis with hips level and body held in its correct relationship to the legs, whether the pelvis is tilted or not, which is turned by the supporting leg. The working leg is merely following the body round – so to speak – therefore its muscles must work as they do in *rond de jambe en l'air*.

At a later stage rotation is performed during a half turn on the *demi-* or full *pointe* or jump. As the chain reaction is quicker the dancer must be sure that the weight is firmly centred over the supporting leg, the waist kept slimmed and the spine held erect until the pelvis "tilts" directly forwards, swiftly and accurately if the raised leg is to be held when it reaches *arabesque*. Rotation *en dedans* (sometimes called *fouetté*) requires the above chain reactions in reverse and as used in *ronds de jambe en l'air dedans*, the utmost care being taken to maintain turn-out because the supporting leg rotates inwards and needs greater control and strength from all the muscles inserting into the hip-socket and the front and back of the pelvis, if the legs are to be kept in their proper relationship.

84

Grands fouettés relevés or *sautés* use exactly the same muscular technique as rotation but must be given strong impetus from a preparatory *grand battement devant* (or *derrière*) which not only raises and holds the working leg at its height, but also lifts the dancer straight upwards into a spring or *relevé* (figure 126). At the height of the jump or *relevé* he or she must turn in the air into *arabesque* before descending *fondu* on the same spot at which the step began. The *arabesque* must be centred over the supporting leg. It is in such movements that a perfect synchronisation and co-ordination of arms and legs will help to control the turn and balance of the finished pose (see p. 84).

11. Petits Ronds de Jambe en l'Air

Strictly speaking *petits ronds de jambe en l'air* belong to the same category as *battements frappés* or *fondus* (see p. 77), i.e. those in which some part of the leg moves independently of the rest of the limb which is held still. But the knee is not only a "hinge", it is capable of some rotation when RELAXED, therefore it is included here. Because of this slight rotation it requires more careful attention than any other joint. Provided the dancer always centres the knee directly under the hip and over the centre of the foot whether the leg is straight or bent, few problems should arise once turn-out is mastered and the relationship of the knee to the direction travelled is understood. But much damage can be done to the knee if the greatest care is not taken as the delicate cartilages can easily tear or slip, as many footballers find to their cost. This is particularly so if *petits ronds de jambe* are used in some jumping step and the dancer does not complete the tiny circling with a completely accurate stretch of the leg outwards from the knee before continuing into the next movement. It is important for the child to understand that a *petit rond*, whether outwards or inwards, should always begin from a fully stretched, turned out leg raised to any height above 30°. The muscles round the knee alone relax and the lower leg circles inwards or outwards before being stretched into the same straight line at the side so that the knee muscles can then lock the two parts of the leg together before proceeding. This locking and circling requires that the upper half of the leg be held immobile by the strength of those same muscles which lift it into any *battement relevé* and, when the leg is bent, into any *retiré*.

VIII. MUSCLES IN GENERAL USE

By the time children have practised the above movements at the barre, they should have some idea of how most of the major muscles work when dancing. They can be broadly summarised.

1. To Attain Stance and to Bend, Stretch and Rotate the Body and Head

The Erector Spinae, the great spinal muscle linking vertebrae to every part of the body from sacrum to head (see pp. 13, 21, 57).

The Lattissimus Dorsi emanate from each side of the spine between the sacrum and thoracic vertebrae, and ascend diagonally outwards passing under the trapezius and shoulder-blades. Some insert in front of the rib-cage below the arms, some into the arm socket (see pp. 19, 21, 55, 56, 57, 63, 64).

The Trapezius arise from the back of the head and insert into the scapula and clavicle thus affecting all the movements of the shoulders and head (see pp. 19, 21, 23, 55, 65).

The Sterno-mastoid link the head to the collar bone and breast bones, beneath them lie other muscles stretching from the skull to the two upper ribs and spine (see pp. 23, 63).

The Deltoid lie across the top of the shoulders linking arm to shoulder and chest (see pp. 21, 55, 65).

The Recti Abdominis are attached to the front of the pelvis and under the lower part of the rib-cage (see pp. 13, 16, 17, 56, 57, 64).

The Psoas emanate from the front of the lumbar vertebrae, pass through the groin to the inner side of the femur (see pp. 53, 71).

All the above with the addition of the Diaphragm, inner and outer intercostal muscles play some part in straightening the four curves of the spine and all but the psoas are controlled or used when breathing correctly (see p. 22, and diagrams 2 and 4).

2. To Bend, Stretch, Raise (Rise) and Rotate the Legs

All the muscles enumerated below are affected by the turn-out of classical dance, as is the *Psoas* (see above). This means that they do not work as in normal movement. The turn-out affects most particularly those muscles linking the whole of the pelvis to the legs at both front and back. They all have to be re-educated to stretch and work so that their new length compensates for the alteration made in the way the legs move, i.e. although the foot and knee no longer face front, they still have to travel forwards, backwards and sideways as in ordinary life, activated by movements taken in the hip-socket by muscles which are holding the thigh in its new relationship to the pelvis. This new relationship dictates the positions and movements in knee and foot. Moreover these muscles must be taught to relax in such a way that they never impede the performance of other leg muscles not so intimately connected with the pelvis, but which also acquire a more sophisticated method of movement.

The Y-Shaped and Pubo-Femoral ligaments are in most need of re-education because they are naturally short and fairly tight. They CANNOT BE STRETCHED, they have therefore to be controlled at their maximum length by muscles round the hip-joint so that the head of the femur can rotate slightly outwards and be held in this new position in the hip-socket with the help of other muscles in the buttocks (see pp. 14, 44, 71, 74, and diagram 3).

The Gracilis links the front of the pelvis to the back of the knee but with the turn-out runs in a more or less straight line down the inside of the upper leg together with the Flexors (see pp. 13, 14, 16, 38, 52, 71).

The Sartorius stretches from the outer edge of the pelvis, passing over the gracilis and wraps round below the knee. It needs extra length to allow it to function properly in its new alignment with the direction travelled (see pp. 13, 14, 15, 16, 38, 52, 67, 71).

The Gluteus Maximus and muscles lying beneath and forming the buttocks link thigh to the back of the pelvis and hip-socket. They must be re-educated to contract and help control the turn-out, but also to stretch to their limit and give length to the leg in its new relationship to the pelvis. They must also be strengthened to help lift the leg to its highest in conjuction with the psoas and biceps (see pp. 13, 21, 52, 56, 65, 69, 70).

The Biceps, semi-tendius and semi-membraneous muscles also link the back of the thigh to the hip-socket and pelvis. They emerge from the so-called hamstrings which stand out behind the knee. They need extra length as they are so intimately connected with the gluteus maximus in lifting the leg and if short, contracted or tensed in any way can prevent the leg being raised as well as the proper relaxation in any *demi-plié*, and also prevent the hip-joint being used to its greatest extent as a "hinge" (see pp. 15, 16, 21, 38, 51, 52, 56, 67, 71).

The Quadriceps link both the upper and lower leg to the front of the pelvis. Because of their particular relationship with the knee and hip-socket, they need length, strength and control so that they can be equally stretched and/or relaxed if they are to play a greater part than merely contracting to hold the leg at its highest. They must never be "bunched" to give strength, they must also be stretched to give length (see pp. 14, 15, 16, 21, 38, 39, 52, 67, 71).

The Gastrocnemius and Soleus form the calf and terminate in the Achilles tendon (tendo calcaneous) which emanates from the heel, thus linking heel to foot and knee. These muscles need to acquire as much flexibility as possible so that they can rapidly stretch and/or contract to give life, strength and speed to every action taking place through foot, instep and ankle (see pp. 14, 38, 56).

The Peroneal, Tibial, Extensor and other muscles linking the front, side and back of the legs and running through the foot under and over the instep and into the toes have already been mentioned (see pp. 15, 16, 38, 57). They need to become as sensitive and pliable as possible to give impetus and strength to the dancer in carrying the weight of the body slowly or swiftly from foot to foot. Above all they must be controlled and used in such a way that no matter at which height the foot is raised, the weight is always carried and correctly centred through the straight line of the spine over the talus, and thus over the longitudinal and transverse arches of the foot, no matter to which height it is raised (see p. 38 and figures 40–60).

IX. THE GIVING OF IMPETUS

When dancing Noverre's seven movements it is more important to interpret their qualities rather than exercise strict muscular discipline. However, because these qualities only show to perfection when there is total co-ordination, it is important to pay attention to which part gives impetus to propel the body and adjust it to the changing *épaulements*, tempi and other elements giving expression to the dance. Earlier it has been noted how wide a range of movement Weaver covered when analysing his four simple muscular activities (see p. 50). They are

Transfer of Weight.

121 Preparatory *Fondu*. Note how Judith has slightly anticipated the forwards movement by the poise of her head and shoulders.

122 *Posé* into a low *arabesque*, which still continues the forwards line, because Judith has concentrated to carry her weight on to the new supporting leg, but has not neglected fully to stretch the back leg and her body into *arabesque*.

still utilised in his way so that BEND is part of the GLIDE of a *chassé*; STRETCH can mean Rise (or raise); RISE can mean to JUMP; and TURN to rotate or circle; i.e. such terms are still used in the class-room. The only term Weaver does not use is DART, but he distinguishes between a swift step flying OVER the ground as opposed to a *chassé* ON the ground and mentions the quick anticipatory action of the head essential to any *élancé* step (i.e. darting). If Noverre's seven movements of dance are to acquire their particular qualities, examination should be made of how to perform them. In most cases this entails a study of how and where to place impetus.

As soon as centre work is practised the student must understand exactly how and where to place the weight of the body and which part will give the necessary impetus to transfer it from one step or pose into the next. Few movements begin without a preparatory *demi-plié* or *fondu*. However although either is sufficient to give impetus to the leg or legs to send the dancer upwards from two feet and return to two as in *soubresauts*; or from one foot to the same as in *temps levé*; or one to the other as in *petits jetés*; if the dancer is using another of the five ways of jumping to travel, or wishes to elaborate the above simple jumps with beats, something more is required. The legs do not always take full responsibility for moving the body from place to place. Often they must be helped by head, arms or body. It is useful therefore to make some analysis of where extra impetus can be given, always remembering that although emphasis may be placed on one or another part, it is only when all are used, all the time, in co-ordination that the dancer becomes an expressive instrument, an interpreter of classical dance.

123 *À côté*. The bodies and heads indicate the line of the *élancé* and are held as the student's land in *fondu*.

124 *En arrière*. Stephen and Judith have sufficient strength to "hold" their bodies at the appropriate angle as they land.

125 *En avant*. Both have stretched their working legs well away from the hip joint to maintain *arabesque* as they land *fondu*.

1. The Impetus Given by the Head

The important part played by the head to give direction and impetus in many types of *cambré* has been noted (see pp. 56–65 and figures 77–92), so has the need to place it slightly behind the direction travelled into a curve for *grand jeté en avant* finishing in *arabesque* (see p. 75). But there are many instances when the head must give impetus. Because it is the heaviest part of the body (it weighs about ten pounds), it must always be correctly poised and given independence to help the dancer move easily and appropriately. The anticipatory movement of the head is evident in figures 70–74 (see p. 40) where it precedes the transfer of the body over to the new supporting leg in *chassé à terre* and during the preliminary *fondu* before a *posé en avant*, so that the weight is already over the spot upon which the supporting leg will poise (figures 121, 122). Such a transfer from a low *fondu* to a position high *sur les pointes* can only be achieved if the weight is correctly centred and held through the spine and legs during the whole movement.

It is during such steps as *sissonnes ouvertes* and *fermées* that the head plays a vital part in giving direction and space to the distance travelled. Simultaneously with the spring out of the *demi-plié*, the dancer must direct the head so that the body inclines at a slight angle and travels sideways, forwards or backwards in the air, legs held together. The angle made allows the about-to-be supporting leg to open slightly and descend under the body in a perpendicular line, the weight being correctly centred when the dancer pauses in *fondu*. As in *grand jeté en avant* the final pose has been anticipated in the air, and needs only to be held as the step is completed (figures 123–125).

89

It is perhaps the action and poise of the head which most distinguishes a darting from a gliding movement if the legs are working correctly. *Èlance* movements are marked by the very swift change in the angle of the head as it leads the body from an upright to an inclined position (see *sissonnes* p. 96), but *glissé* steps should find the hips and shoulders level and square to some front, the head either facing forwards or turning towards the direction travelled (i.e. *glissade devant* or *derrière*). However the true quality of any *glissade* lies in the action of the legs. The step can be small and very dainty, or cover space with strong action, but it should always be smooth and steady and the action equally balanced because both legs are responsible for carrying the body from one spot to the other, particularly if the *glissade* is a preparation for some step of grand *elevation*. If the *glissade* is not along the floor, the height of the following jump loses effect. It is often the swift change in the poise of the head which can make such steps as *temps de cuisse* exciting. For example, the first *retiré passé* may require a turned head and glance downwards at the working leg immediately followed by a stretch upwards and backwards glance to coincide with the *sissonne dessus*.

Sometimes it is the sheer weight of the head pressing downwards through the spine on to the leading foot before a big jump that gives sufficient impetus and strength for the dancer to double the effort of springing upwards as the working leg is thrown into *grand battement devant* as the first part of a *fouetté sauté*. However a word of warning should be given before practising ways of placing extra weight on the leading foot in *grand elevation*. They should never be too minutely analysed, nor performed in slow motion, but so timed that the extra pressure brought to bear is scarcely visible and the spring from the *fondu* is all but simultaneous. It is the LIFT into the air that matters, not the downwards pressure into the floor that makes that spring possible (figure 126).

The head plays its most important part during *pirouettes*. In these it must always move freely and accurately as it swiftly turns to focus and re-focus the "spot" or "spots" at which the *pirouette* begins and ends. Its action must be carefully timed to give the entire central line of the body impetus to turn in one piece. The tiny movement the head makes from one side to the other and which is then held focussing the "spot" must be swift enough to reinforce the movement of the supporting leg. But to achieve this satisfactorily its action must also coincide exactly with the rise out of the preparation, the lift of the working leg into the appropriate position, the intake of breath, the closing of both arms into 1st or 5th (or other pose) and the "force" given by the shoulder of the arm coming into the turn (figures 127–129).

2. The Impetus Given by the Arms

The part played by the shoulder to give "force" in a *pirouette* is very difficult to analyse, because the extra pressure brought to bear upon the torso by the arm coming into the turn should be all but invisible. Moreover it should be so timed that it comes immediately after the rise or *relevé* to demi- or full *pointe* and the appropriate lift of the working leg, making the audience aware only of the *pirouette* and not the details of the preparation. Nevertheless students should under-

126 The leg is thrown up in *grand battement devant* before the turn into *arabesque* in a *fouetté*. Note the erect back as Judith directs the leg forwards.

stand how to bring "force" behind the shoulder coming into the turn at the same moment of breathing in quickly with the stretch upwards out of the preparation. To do this they should remember to make their intake of breath strong and deep enough, just after both arms are opened to 2nd, to be held firmly as they are brought together in a shortened 1st. The lungs are thus expanded sideways and give the lattissimus dorsi, trapezius and other respiratory muscles room to hold the spine erect, both shoulder-blades open and away from the rib-cage, which is held upwards by the recti abdominis. The tiny movement giving "force" to the arm coming into the turn with the intake of breath must be strong, accurate and swift because it occurs only in the upper arm and must coincide with a similar but slightly weaker movement from the other arm.

This tiny movement to give "force" is best practised standing back to a wall, feet in 1st position, arms in 2nd, the dancer feeling that the body from elbow to elbow is nearly flat, but not touching the wall. Firstly the weight must be correctly centred and forwards; and secondly the elbows must not fall behind the shoulders. From this position bring only the lower arms towards each other, but when they are about to form an angle, gently press the upper arms inwards (without moving the shoulders at all) thus creating a shortened but rounded 1st position as if gathering everything together round the centre line of balance. It is this tiny movement of the upper arms bringing pressure to bear on the small curve thus formed that gives sufficient "force" to start the *pirouette* in motion. The head then takes over the turn by its swift twist to re-focus the "spot". Once this tiny movement has been mastered it has to be so accurately timed and smoothly performed that it can be used just after the dancer has risen from the preparation, breath held, eyes focussing front. Then after a fraction of delay in a pose – so to speak – the arms move towards each other and the extra pressure helps the dancer to gather all his limbs and muscles together for the *pirouette* (figures 127–129).

In classical dance the arms and shoulders should never be seen obviously to give impetus. If too much force is put into such movements it too easily distorts the line or pulls the shoulders out of place. Nevertheless arms must be so co-ordinated with the rest of the body that the dancer maintains the necessary aplomb during most difficult steps. The "force" brought to bear by the shoulder coming into the *pirouette* is the only occasion when it is so used, and if this tiny movement is analysed it will be found that it is the strong action of the muscles in the upper arm which brings the necessary pressure to bear on the torso and makes it turn. This will only be successful if the arms work in isolation and happens when the deltoid, latissimus dorsi and trapezius muscles are firmly controlled to hold the shoulder-blades still as well as the spine erect over the centre of balance, and the head is freed from tension by similar control over the accessory respiratory and other muscles holding the rib-cage and neck.

In most types of jump the impetus to rise upwards and/or along comes principally from the action of the legs and feet. Their movement should be rein-forced by a somewhat similar action from the arms bringing pressure to bear against the air and helping to lift and carry the body up and/or along.

The basic rule that the same arm as the foot closing in front during such steps as *glissades*, *sissonnes* and *assemblés* introduces one of the most important elements in *elevation* (see p. 38) namely: open the arms during a travelling step to give it an air of spaciousness, but close one or the other on completion of the step to stabilise balance when the feet return to the floor. Moreover if one or both arms commence from a closed position, then the opening of an arm coinciding with the upwards and/or outwards thrust of the leg (legs) helps to propel the dancer against the forces of gravity (see p. 42). The need to press against these forces and the "feel" of the arms being lifted from beneath as the body rises into the air, helped by an intake of breath gives the dancer extra strength, particularly if the torso is held by all the same muscles controlling the spine, head and rib-cage as in a *pirouette*. In addition, the moment the feet leave the floor in any kind of jump the body should be held still until they return and the step is finished (see p. 37).

The reason for keeping the body absolutely still during the flight through the air, or during a *pirouette* arises because the dancer has to combat the forces of gravity. This phenomena can roughly be explained thus: the preparatory arm and leg (or both) must press upwards and/or along with sufficient strength simultane-ously with the spring or rise (*relevé*) and intake of breath pushing the weight of the air away from the body, thus momentarily creating a vacuum within which to travel or rise more easily before the forces of gravity again descend. Thus in a *pirouette* the dancer creates a vacuum within which to turn by opening and then swiftly closing the arms, gathering all forces together to spin before the arms open and the weight of the air again descends (see p. 42). Dancers should remember therefore that the higher they rise on the supporting foot and the more compactly

Pirouette.

127 Preparation *pointe tendue* side.

128 *Demi-plié* in closed 4th, note shortening of front arm.

129 *Pirouette,* at the moment when the turn begins. Stephen's arms are in shortened 1st, his working leg in *retiré* and the supporting foot has risen and begun to turn. But the head "spots" the same front as in preparation above. Note how the weight is centred.

93

they balance their bodies over the centre, the less pressure there will be from the forces of gravity and thus the easier it will be to turn.

A similar forming of "a vacuum in which to jump" is needed in *grands jetés en tournant*, *grands fouettés sautés* and other steps of elevation. If a full *ports de bras* is used, the arms should open to 2nd position as the leading foot is pressed into the floor by the weight of the body which is directed downwards by the head. They then descend to *bras bas* very swiftly, and simultaneously with the spring upwards ascend to 5th. At the height of the jump and immediately with the turn in the air, they open again to 2nd. The arms thus opening on either side of the body help the dancer to regain equilibrium and withstand the forces of gravity.

The above only serves as one example of the simplest way of using the arms to give impetus in *grand elevation* because it illustrates the need always to analyse carefully the *ports de bras* for any type of jump to help to increase its height, length breadth and depth.

3. The Impetus Given by the Legs

Children frequently fail to use the floor firmly enough when first studying, particularly when transferring weight from one foot to the other (see pp. 40, 42). This weakens much *terre à terre* work and the lack of firm contact with what should be the spring-board becomes more obvious when the student begins to jump and travel in some direction no matter which of the five jumps is being used.

X. FIVE ESSENTIAL RULES FOR JUMPS

The impetus that can be given by the legs and feet for a jump has been briefly stated (see p. 69), but further analysis is needed if the basic barre-work is to be practised correctly in the centre. Firstly: care must be taken to place the weight appropriately during the preparation. All too often too little weight is directed either over the supporting leg (legs) before it springs up or along; or the body has been inadequately directed to travel in a certain way (see p. 89). Secondly: insufficient emphasis is made upon the type and area of impetus needed to give each of the five forms of jump its particular quality. The following serve as essential rules, but as work becomes more advanced, details are bound to change.

1. Jumps from Two Feet to Two Feet

When jumping from and returning to two feet in one of the five positions e.g. *changements*, *soubresauts*, *échappés* etc, the weight must be placed centrally and equally over the two feet in *demi-plié* so that they give impetus and together push the body upwards in a straight line. It is now essential that the muscular chain reaction for descending and ascending in *demi-pliés* is used (see p. 51). If however the dancer uses the full depth of the *demi-plié* and then exerts a little more pressure this will make the feet react strongly and raise the body higher in the air. If – as so often happens in choreography – the dancer has to travel forwards or backwards with feet together e.g. *soubresauts*, it is usually sufficient to direct the head appropriately towards the path of travel (figures 130, 131).

94

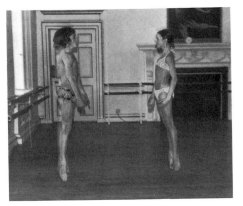

Jumps in 1st.

130 Correct jump in 1st, but Judith's arms are too far behind her shoulders.

131 Incorrect jumps in 1st. Stephen has thrown his weight back and Judith has not stretched her spine upwards.

Although *glissades* are not true jumping steps, it is important to understand that whether they have to cover a short or long distance, both legs are equally responsible for carrying the dancer over the ground. The distance to be travelled is determined by the depth of the *demi-plié*, the length of the stretch to *pointe tendue* and the strength of the spring from the supporting leg. If the distance is short scarcely any *demi-plié* is needed, in a series of *glissades sur les pointes* none is used. If however it is large, then there must be a stronger stretch to *pointe tendue* from a deeper *demi-plié*. There will be a higher spring upwards and outwards from the supporting leg, lifting the body and therefore the pointed toe higher from the floor. The dancer then has to follow a longer line downwards from the originally pointed toe before closing the feet. If the legs and shoulders are kept level and facing the same plane during the transfer of weight, the action of the legs will be equalised and the balance of the body stabilised during its flight (see p. 88).

2. From One Foot to Two Feet

The most important decision to make when jumping from one foot to both, as in *assemblés* is whether to travel or not. Although *assemblés en place* and *portés* (travelled) commence from a similar preparation i.e. the supporting leg is always *fondu* after the initial *demi-plié* and finish with the stretched legs joined in the air before descending together, there is a subtle difference in the amount and placing of the impetus given to the jump. This largely depends upon the timing of the movements before the spring. If the *assemblé* is to be *en place*, then the extension along the floor to *pointe tendue* should be completed simultaneously with the spring from the supporting foot. This spring carries the body upwards only and at the height of the jump the opened leg must be brought inwards so that both legs can descend together. The impetus for an *assemblé porté* must however be given a deeper *demi-plié* and a stronger extension to *pointe tendue*, which is completed a fraction of a second before the spring upwards and along. This action is more like that of a *battement frappé* because it requires some friction to lift the working leg, thus strengthening the spring which should be such that it, not only raises the body, but also propels it through the air, bringing it into a perpendicular position over the spot originally indicated by the pointed toe (see p. 77). At the height of the jump the leg making the jump – so to speak – joins its fellow in the air and both descend together. The arms can play a vital part if they open widely with the legs in any *assemblé porté*, particularly if it has to be *en tournant* (see p. 91).

3. Two Feet to One Foot

Any type of *sissonne* serves as an example of jumping from two feet to one foot, because all demand that the original impetus to spring comes from both feet equally no matter whether the *sissonne* is *en place* (i.e. *ordinaire*, *simple* or *petite*) or travelled. Similarly both legs should be kept closed tightly until the height of the jump and only after that does the transfer of weight to the about-to-be supporting leg takes place. *Sissonnes ordinaires* or *simples* require impetus and a spring upwards from both legs, then just as the tips of the toes are about to touch the floor, one or the other foot is raised into a *retiré* or pose appropriate to the following step. The weight of the body now being firmly centred over one leg *fondu*. All other *sissonnes* finishing *fermées* or *ouvertes* require the same impetus given by both legs from the *demi-plié*, but as stated earlier, the impetus to travel depends upon the dancer's understanding of how to give direction by the correct placing of the head and body (see p. 89 and figures 123–125).

4. From One Foot to the Other

Jetés of all kinds require a similar technique as used when transferring weight from one foot to the other in *chassé à terre* (see p. 40). Nevertheless great care must be taken when transferring weight in the air so that it is always centred at the height of the jump. In *petits jetés*, which only travel a short distance backwards or forwards when danced *en place*, the working foot should always be brought back under the central line of balance before it descends to the floor simultaneously with the lift of the other leg to *retiré* (see p. 40). The height of the *petit jeté* varies a great deal and depends upon the amount of friction made by the working foot as it "swishes" out sideways to give impetus to the spring from the supporting leg. In some cases however the outwards "swish" is not used, nor is it in some *petits jetés en tournant*, this means that the dancer has to rely on the strength of each leg working independently to keep the body rising and falling at the same height and speed. In all such movements breath control is most important.

As mentioned earlier when practising *grands jetés en avant* the first aim should be to determine which type is needed. The use of the head to direct the line for a romantic curving leap has been mentioned (see p. 75). In a modern "split" *jeté* the dancer must direct the head and body straight forwards indicating the line to be travelled simultaneously with the spring from the floor, open the legs and endeavour to keep both at the same height whilst travelling through the air. If the *jeté* is to end in *arabesque* the pose will only be possible of performance after the supporting foot reaches the floor. During the flight the dancer should appear to be

96

"cutting" through the air. A somewhat similar technique is required for the so-called "flick" or *développé jeté*. The dancer springs into the air with the front leg bent and straightens it at the height of the jump to land as in the above "split" *jeté*. It should be noted that a "flick" *jeté* should not be attempted from a turned-out *retiré*. The dancer raises the bent leg in front of the body as he or she soars into the air and is thus given greater strength to cut through the forces of gravity.

5. Jumps on One Foot Only

Temps levés requires the weight to be absolutely centred on one and the same supporting and springing foot so firmly that the dancer maintains the required pose for as long as necessary. These movements depend entirely upon the strength and ability of that whole leg to stretch and relax slowly or quickly, or even erratically to keep the dancer bouncing – as it were – in the air. Because *temps levés* are used so often as preparatory movements as well as steps in their own right, children should be taught early to lift themselves from the floor until the fully stretched leg and pointed toe are seen to rise and stretch lightly and then relax and fall softly only to rebound again and again to keep the dancer moving. Such is the art of *balon*, without which any dance seems earth-bound.

4

DIFFERENCES BETWEEN THE MALE AND FEMALE DANCER

IT is perhaps too often forgotten in countries whose school of classical dance is still in a formative stage that although there may be little difference in the physical shape of the boy and girl before they begin to develop, teachers must build for the future during the first days of training. They must ensure that neither boy nor girl acquires technical habits and movements which rightly belongs to the opposite sex. Students of classical dance, particularly teenagers, should not be taught together in the daily class until such time as their basic technique is firmly established and their figures are all but fully grown (figures 132–134).

The first difference to take into consideration is the purely physical shape of the children's bodies. The boy's spine is usually straighter, his hips narrower and his shoulders broader than a girl's (figures 1–12), and when fully grown he tends to be taller than a girl of the same age. This is important because in double-work (*pas de deux*) if the girl, standing *sur les pointes*, is taller than her partner, he will find it difficult to give her full support when balancing, in *pirouettes* or when lifting her weight.

Because the boy usually has greater height, his muscles are generally longer to move this extra length and weight of the bones in limbs and body. But care must be taken when strengthening his muscles that they are not allowed to "bunch" by being constantly tensed so that he becomes muscle bound. This easily happens if too much attention is paid to holding the legs at some height by contracting the quadriceps and calf muscles, and not enough to stretching the gluteus maximus, biceps, sartorius and gracilis. The boy should spend more time studying how to equalise the tension and relaxation of his muscles, particularly when he begins to grow and often loses control and the strength of his limbs at the hip-joints – unlike the girl who tends to slacken at the waist and in the spine when at the same stage of growth.

Admittedly this equalisation of tension and relaxation at the hip-joints, is sometimes difficult to achieve because the boy's hips, being narrower than a girl's, means that the turn-out is not so easy to manage. The Y-shaped and pubo-femoral ligaments are not any longer than a girl's in proportion to the extra length of a boy's legs. Therefore the narrower hips, flatter pelvis and longer femur ought, but seldom do, to have a greater capacity for rotating outwards in this area (see p. 14). Moreover there is another problem more frequently met with amongst boys than girls. The legs of a boy studying classical dance frequently seem to grow

98

132 Students are able to balance on *demi-pointes* if the spine remains erect and centred over the insteps.

133 The growing boy and girl showing the difference in stance. Judith is poised but a little more forwards than Stephen.

134 On *demi-pointes*. Judith has now stretched to her fullest in order to centre her weight more firmly.

faster than the rest of his body. This means that before the muscles holding his spine, pelvis and rib-cage correctly over the centre of balance are fully stretched and strengthened, they are having to cope with the extra weight and length of his legs and feet. It is for this reason that it is always best never to allow a boy's legs to be lifted or thrown above 90° before he can control his spine and pelvis. It is at this stage also that a boy fails to appreciate his rate of growth and tends to drop his head, thus his eye level is down. He must be encouraged to stretch upwards through the cervical vertebrae and hold his head up without tensing his chin, otherwise he tends to round his shoulders and drop his chest instead of broadening the line of his torso by stretching the latissimus dorsi, trapezius and recti abdominis upwards. Above all the spine must be straight, strong and very much held by all these muscles from the pelvis to under the shoulder-blades. He must also feel as if these same muscles run in continuous lines from the spine to the shoulders, chest and beneath the arms, so that he can feel not only how to lift his own arms, but also the girl, when required by a choreographer.

The boy must learn to control his limbs in the earliest stages of training because the basic shape of his body is not going to change very much. He will never acquire the extra weight of bust and buttocks like a girl, and even if – as in England – he loses his "baby tummy" later than elsewhere, it is essential that he understands where the centre of balance must lie at every stage in class (figure 127).

Boys usually do find it more difficult to control the recti abdominis than girls, but they must be encouraged to stretch these muscles upwards at all times when straightening the spine, therefore the first consideration should be for him to take correct stance, so that he is always aware how to straighten by stretching upwards and how to use the three curves of the spine. To do this he will have to learn how to utilise the thoracic and cervical vertebrae and head to keep him on balance. Correct stance, once established, must be constantly stressed. Once stance has become habitual it is very difficult to change, therefore much hard work can be eliminated if stance is correct from the beginning. The girl also has to stretch and straighten her spine before her bust and buttocks begin to develop, but when these increase in size with growth she must adjust and strengthen the action of the abdominal and diaphragm muscles in front of the body and the gluteus maximus and muscles lying beneath at the back to cope with their extra weight, which unfortunately is mostly fat. To adjust successfully means that she must carefully stretch the head to re-centre it over the line of balance and the three points of the foot. If she does not pay attention to this her weight will not be correctly placed (see p. 14 and figures 133, 134).

This is not to say that the boy's weight is further back than a girl's. Far from it, because he needs a far stronger, straighter spine in the lumbar and thoracic regions than a girl if he is going to be an adequate partner for any type of double-work. He must always be able to keep his own weight correctly centred as well as that of his partner, whether she is balancing with his help on a flat foot (figure 130) or *sur les pointes* in some pose, or lifting her. If his weight is too far back he can damage his lumbar vertebrae, groin or knees very seriously as well as upset the girl's balance and probably nerve. In addition he must, as a partner, realise his own capacity to stretch leg, arm or body in any direction without losing control or balance for much double-work depends upon the boy's ability to counter-balance the girl's weight as she falls or moves into some pose as he takes another.

Other differences arise because of the squarer shoulders of the boy which makes it easier for him to raise his arms directly over his head in 5th, provided he does not bring his fingers too close together when circling them upwards. Never-theless he should always follow the classical rule that the arms never go behind the shoulder and if his finger-tips are the width of his forehead apart in 5th; in *bras bas*, they should also be the width between the centre of his knees apart. This measure-ment should be taken by each boy for himself. If used correctly it forms an excellent guide to keep his shoulders square and firmly opened. He should constantly practise the circling of the arms mentioned in the section on *ports de bras* (see p. 56) as this will help him to maintain the necessary turn of the hand as it ascends or descends without fuss. Moreover by paying constant attention to keeping the shoulders open the boy acquires a valuable attribute when lifting a girl to sit on his shoulder as he is then able to lift his head comfortably to look upwards. If he does not have freedom of the head and arms, this cannot happen.

The girl's arms are not held directly above the head in 5th position because in so doing it would throw her weight too far backwards and probably protrude her chest. When raising them to 5th she should be able to glance into the palms of her hands and if she maintains the same relationship of her arms to her body when she lowers them to *bras bas*, they will be further away from her body than the boy's. These positions of the girl's arms not only give them a more rounded, softer line than a boy's, but are essential in double-work. If her arms are too far back, so will be her weight and this will immediately affect both her own and her partner's balance. Moreover if they are too straight, particularly if stretched too far forwards in a *pirouette*, he cannot remain close enough to catch her firmly on completion of the turn, and by having to grab – so to speak – after having stepped back to avoid the outstretched arms, is likely to pull her off balance.

The teacher should bear in mind when first teaching boys that if and when he reaches professional status he will be expected to excel in two particular types of step namely; *pirouettes* and *grand elevation* with or without *batterie*. It is useful therefore to spend more time on the basic exercises for such movements than on elaborate *ports de bras* and long *adages*. Work on *ports de bras* must not be neglected. The need to stress the breadth of the arm movement, a masculine looking hand (figure 135) and a strong fully stretched back has been noted. But the boy must spend a long time studying the synchronisation of his arms with the legs and body as they occur in every preparation for a *pirouette, tour en l'air* and *grand elevation*, and the need to hold the arms absolutely still in position at the height of the movement. A boy too often flings his shoulders into a movement rather than keeping them firmly controlled. Like the girl he should understand the placing of the arms on either side of the central line so that he achieves equality of movement, particularly when he balances after some big jump in so sophisticated a pose as the *attitude* (figures 136, 137).

It is always useful to remind the boy that, like the girl, he must always breathe in and stretch upwards before any back bend. But because he does not need the flexibility of a girl, he should not attempt to curve his spine below the 7th thoracic vertebrae, thus avoiding any arching of the back at the waist-line, a thing that can be dangerous when lifting a girl as this throws too much weight on his knees instead of it being spread and held over his central line of balance, the straight and strong spine.

Another valuable movement to strengthen and achieve a greater turn-out is to encourage the boy to attempt both *demi-* and full *pliés* from a wider 2nd position than the conventional measurement allows. i.e. The feet should be the length of one of the performer's own feet apart. Instead he should stretch out as far as possible in a *battement tendu* to the side and then extend the toe outwards a little further till the distance is two feet lengths apart. If there is correct relaxation and contraction at the hip-joints during the descent and ascent from this larger position, it will help him to rotate the head of the femur a little further in the hip-socket thus freeing the Y-shaped and pubo-femoral ligaments a little and stretching the sartorius and gracilis and adductors. It also gives him greater breadth and depth of movement to stretch the rest of his leg muscles both passively and actively (see p. 51).

Another important item when teaching boys is to insist that they work on both legs at the same time, particularly when working quickly. Too often attention

135 *Arabesque penché.* With Stephen's help Judith is stretching her body downwards at an angle to her supporting leg.

136 *Attitude croisé devant.* Note slight tilt forwards of pelvis and stretch upwards of the body from the waist.

137 Back view to show centre line of balance from the crown of the head through to the foot.

is concentrated on the working leg, the supporting leg being left to take care of itself. This is also true of some girls' work. But it is vital for boys to realise the need to stabilise weight correctly over the supporting leg at all times because his legs are not usually as loose as a girl's, he therefore tends to throw himself off balance in his efforts to raise or hold his leg as high as possible. It is also vital because if he is unable to stabilise balance – particularly when working quickly and transferring his weight from one foot to the other, his work both as a dancer and partner will not acquire the necessary aplomb. Uncertainty of balance in a male dancer is far more noticeable than in a girl for the audience expects him to look stronger and more assured if his dance is to be masculine in quality.

The need to give strength to the spine and breadth to the boy's shoulders has been noted (see p. 100) and this is where the strongest difference has to be made when teaching the boy and girl their appropriate rôles in double-work. It is not the purpose of this book to analyse the various balances and lifts. There is only space to offer a few comments because it cannot be too strongly stressed that both are responsible for making a success of any movement in *pas de deux*.

1. Boy and girl must learn to adapt their movements to each other, whilst at the same time remembering the basic rules of classical dance (see pp. 46–50).

2. If they both breathe in with the effort they will more easily achieve the desired result.

(*a*) The boy will more easily find the level and shape of his partner's waist and thus the shape his hands must take to hold his partner firmly on completion of the movement if the girl, in particular, breathes in strongly as she rises into the *pirouette*.

(*b*) If the girl's breath is held at the moment a pose is taken, perhaps after a *posé* into *attitude* or *arabesque*, he has a better opportunity to grasp the proffered hand at the height of the movement and thus help her to retain that pose more firmly during his walk round, or give her more confidence if she has to move from one pose to another.

(*c*) If both breathe in firmly at the moment of the lift away from the floor, whether the girl springs or not, the filling of the lungs with air not only makes her lighter, but gives him greater strength for the lift because his chest is firmly stretched outwards and his shoulders held.

3. Once a pose is taken, either when balancing after a *posé* or *pirouette*, or in the air during a jump, the girl must remain perfectly still as during any jump in *grand elevation* (see p. 93). There should only be some relaxation during any lift if there is to be a shift from one pose to another, but only of the appropriate part or parts of the body. The girl must never allow herself to become a dead weight, except in rare circumstances demanded by a particular rôle.

4. In addition to any ruling that may be decided by the couple when performing any of the above types of movement, they must always be certain of the exact direction the step or lift must take, and make the lines of travel absolutely accurate whether these coincide, converge or part. This means that they must never over-cross the lines of their own legs, arms, heads or bodies, or above all, the line of direction to be travelled together or separately. They must always make for the most economical way of performing a step or lift, eliminating all fussy movement and fidgeting for position, which can happen if either partner has not formed the correct preparation and has to move foot, arm or even the preparation itself before the desired movement begins. Fokine said: "A *pas de deux* in classical dance should be a love poem for two dancers loving that form of dance, not a quarrel or contest between ill-sorted technicians."

5

PROBLEMS ARISING FROM PHYSICAL ANOMALIES
IN CHILDREN

B ECAUSE many injuries arise from incorrect stance teachers should always be alert to correct any mistakes in the placing of a child's limbs, body or head as he or she grows and develops. Incorrect stance causes an improper distribution of weight and this can lead to pain in the lumbar region, groin, knees and/or ankles and feet. But other injuries can arise from physical anomalies, which only disclose themselves as the child progresses in dance. Some can be overcome by careful training always provided there is no abnormality of bone structure or muscular lesion. Anything of that nature is outside the competence of the dancing teacher and must be dealt with by the appropriate orthopedic or medical expert.

One of the first things to note when teaching classical dance is that if an injury occurs, for example on the right side of the body, it seems almost inevitable that a compensatory movement is made on the left. This often leads to strain, even injury in a part distant from the source of trouble, which may finally be more difficult to put right than the original injury. This type of compensatory movement is easy to detect in: 1. children having one leg shorter than the other; 2. Having a slight curvature of the spine; 3. Having an unequal shoulder level.

I. ANOMALIES HINDERING THE DEVELOPMENT OF CORRECT STANCE

1. An Unequal Length of Leg

This anomaly is often due to uneven growth, the child usually sinking into the hip of the longer leg. By thus shortening it the child is then unable to balance satisfactorily when using the longer as the supporting leg because the weight is not correctly held upwards through the spine and the pelvis is not stabilised firmly by the appropriate muscles, which maintain the relationship between the spine and the two legs. Moreover the child will also have difficulty in raising the longer leg to the same height as the shorter one when using the latter as a support, because the muscles in the longer one have not been re-educated to stretch as fully as possible and those in the hip-joint and pelvis have not been sufficiently strengthened.

This anomaly is comparatively easy to detect as the level of the hip is uneven and it is simple to confirm the fault by measuring and comparing the length of each leg from the outer edge of the hip to the inside centre of the ankle. Provided the teacher is sure that unequal length of leg is the reason why the child does not work adequately much can be done to rectify this anomaly – if it is only a minor defect.

The child should be persuaded to stretch correctly upwards on the longer side from the hip-joint at the same time as stretching all the muscles on the shorter side downwards into the leg from the hip-joint to ankle, and upwards from the hip-joint to under the arm-pit. If the arm on the shorter side is held in 5th position during much of the barre-work, this can be helpful.

2. Slight Curvature

As there are several different kinds of curvature, teachers should always seek expert advice when noticing any inequality of movement in the spine and vertebrae. A great deal can be done to help a child with slight curvature by insisting that all the basic rules of ordinary class-work are correctly followed (pp. 47–50). Attention can be paid to one or another set of muscles by relaxing, stretching and strengthening them until the desired result is achieved by careful adjustment and exercise. But teachers should always remember that the adjustment and re-education of one set of muscles in any part of the body will always affect those in another part. Any correction to be made should therefore be carefully considered in relation to the effect it may have elsewhere, and measures taken to co-ordinate the total action of all the muscles in the affected part, or parts, with all the other muscles.

3. An Uneven Shoulder Line

Although an uneven shoulder line may be due to some curvature, it is sometimes due to the child carrying a heavy bag of school books always on the same shoulder or hand. The first thing is to insist that the weight of this bag should be evenly distributed between both shoulders or hands, and an attempt made to encourage the child to stretch upwards all the latissimus dorsi and trapezius muscles in order to raise the sunken shoulder. As with the unequal length of leg, working at the barre with the lower shouldered arm in 5th position is a great help.

In all the above three cases the child can also be helped to "feel" the straight line through the spine and the equalisation of the hip and shoulder levels. This is best done by allowing him or her to lie flat on the floor, the teacher then straightening the spine and equalising the level of hip and shoulder. Even after this has been done the child will frequently insist that he or she is "crooked", and it may take some time and much persuasion for such a child to retain the "feel" of a correct upright and equalised stance when rising to the feet.

One of the great faults in the teaching of classical dance is to develop strong muscles without stretching them, particularly those of the legs. It is not enough to strengthen the muscles and get them to co-ordinate harmoniously with each other. They must all be re-educated to develop slowly the maximum extent of their muscular stretch. To do this they must learn also to relax. The very fact of allowing children to lie straight on the floor in a relaxed state whilst the teacher attempts actively to straighten a spine or adjust the level of hips or shoulders can do a great deal to help children with some physical problem. The teacher can show the children how to isolate then adjust a certain movement or muscles before standing up and actively making the correction for themselves. However the teacher must never use force, this can only damage the tender fibres within the muscles. The younger the child, the worse the damage, particularly if strong movements are made to enforce turn-out.

II. ANOMALIES PREVENTING AN ADEQUATE DEMI-PLIÉ

4. The Tight Achilles Tendon

The first lessons to create a proper understanding of turn-out should concentrate on the *demi-plié* as this is the simplest exercise to re-educate all the leg muscles, making them move in their new direction at the same time as they easily relax and/or stretch without any undue strain being placed elsewhere. The lack of depth in a child's *demi-plié* is not always due to a tight Achilles tendon as is often thought. Undoubtedly this anomaly does occur and the teacher is wiser to encourage the child to relax the knees as far as possible before raising the heels and descending into a full *plié*. A little more depth can be acquired if the weight is brought well forwards, but on no account should any force be used to increase the depth of a *demi-plié*. Instead it is best in such cases to exercise the foot and ankle, making these as flexible as possible so that they respond more readily to the demands for quick reactions when jumping. Moreover, short Achilles tendons are often accompanied by short muscles under the instep, which means that there can be a very swift, jerky rise to three-quarter *pointe* as the heels leave the floor instead of a gradual rise through quarter and *demi-pointe*. This jerky rise can be dangerous, particularly if it occurs during the descent from a jump, when the knee is liable to absorb the shock of the foot's impact on the floor, instead of the shock passing through the whole foot and ankle before rising through the bones of the leg to the knee and hip-joint.

5. Tight Ankle-joints

The lack of a good *demi-plié* may be due however to tight ankle-joints in which the muscles do not relax and stretch sufficiently when the heels leave the floor or return to the ground. This anomaly usually occurs because the muscles, particularly in front of the ankle are short. Such a condition is difficult to rectify, as is the short Achilles tendon. Once again the teacher should ensure that the weight is correctly centred and well forwards over the feet, cultivating as far as possible the flexibility of the muscles in the knees, insteps, metatarsal arches and toes which will need extra care (because such children, although having good looking feet often have difficulty in pointing them, the muscles under the instep also being short as a rule). This type of stiff ankle often seems to go with a slightly longer upper leg, therefore attention should be paid to maintaining an appropriate turn-out during any *plié* to ensure that the straight lines of the legs are directly centred through the bones from the hip-joints to the middle of the feet. This centering of the lines of balance early in training is of particular importance to people with stiff ankles, because, like those with short muscles under the instep, they sometimes have unusual powers of *elevation*.

106

6. Very High Insteps

Another anomaly frequently occurs amongst those students having very high insteps, whose muscles under the longitudinal arch are extremely short and therefore difficult to stretch and relax adequately. Such children usually fail to work on *demi-pointe*, preferring to sustain their weight on three-quarter *pointe* when they rise. In fact like those with short Achilles tendons, they nearly always fail to rise through the foot at all, moving directly with a jerk from the flat to three-quarter height. The teacher should do everything possible to encourage such children to use the *demi-pointe* at all times. This will give their feet greater flexibility and will strengthen the muscles both under the instep and toes and round the ankles. It should also prevent the child placing the weight too far backwards when first rising through the feet on turned-out legs (sometimes that is common amongst such children).

7. Long or Short Toes

It is rare that a child with long or short toes and no other anomaly has much difficulty when performing *pliés*. Occasionally a child is found with a very short little toe and if he or she is not taught early to centre the weight correctly through the middle of the foot, it is very difficult to correct the line of the leg later in training because, in the child's efforts to keep the little toe-joint on the floor when lifting the heel, either when moving into a *plié* or rising on to the toes, the muscles on the outside of the ankle have been over-stretched thus preventing those on the inside being strengthened because they have been tensed to hold the talus firmly over the arches of the foot (see p. 34). Oddly enough children with an extra long big toe and no other anomaly, seldom have difficulty with *pliés* if they are carefully guided to maintain the centre line of the legs as they descend and ascend. Their problems arrive when having to maintain balance on three-quarter *pointe* and particularly when girls begin to dance *sur les pointes*. It is now that the fitting of the *pointe* shoe becomes all important.

8. Cramping the Toes

Strong muscles under the foot are anatomically desirable, but as mentioned above can prevent the foot from being fully pointed. It is essential therefore that at all times to ensure that no child works in shoes which prevent the foot from being fully stretched. In other words, at no times should a child's toes appear to be cramped longways or sideways when he or she takes the weight of the body over the metatarsal arches in *fondu* or *demi-plié*. It is at this point that the toes of the supporting foot (or feet) should be seen to spread (figures 75, 76). If the toes are unable to spread at this moment, tension is bound to occur either in the instep, ankle or even as high as the knee for unless the muscles in front of the ankle are fully relaxed so that the talus balances centrally over the arches of the foot, a compensatory movement will take place elsewhere to keep this vital bone in place.

9. Tight Ham-strings

Tight ham-strings can affect the depth of the *demi-plié*, in which case the teacher should proceed in the same way as when dealing with tight Achilles tendons. But much greater emphasis should be put upon the correct placing of the spine and shoulders. As mentioned earlier (see p. 21) the ham-strings insert into exactly the same area where some vital muscles emerge to hold the spine and rib-cage in place. It is therefore most important that this area be made spacious to allow all these muscles as much freedom as possible to stretch and relax. The first thing to ensure is that the recti abdominis are stretched and held upwards, the latissimus dorsi and trapezius stretched diagonally upwards and outwards from the spine to under the shoulder-blades and arm-pits, and the diaphragm and other respiratory muscles correctly regulate the action of the rib-cage. The child should also be encouraged to "feel" the extra length needed at the back of the leg by giving exercises at the barre which entail stretching all the muscles in the upper leg downwards from the hip-joint to knee. e.g. *Battements tendus* to the side followed by an attempt to drop the heel in 2nd position without transferring weight on to the two feet; or *battements tendus* to the side then turning the foot upwards at the ankle before returning to *pointe tendue* and closing in position.

However it is the flexibility of the lumbar and lower thoracic regions which are most affected by tight ham-strings, therefore the teacher should encourage the child to gain as much flexibility as possible by practising *cambrés* 1, 2, 3–5 and 6 (see pp. 56–66).

Short Achilles tendons can also be the reason why dancers possessing this anomaly find it difficult to give height to their *développés*. It is possible to increase the height to some degree in front and at the side by raising the knee a little before unfolding the leg from *retiré* as mentioned earlier (see p. 78). But when practising this type of *développé,* the greatest care must be taken to hold the muscles controlling spine and pelvis very firmly and correctly, and eliminate any suggestion that the "tail is being tucked in" as this either throws the weight too far back or the dancer uses the pelvis and lower vertebrae to help lift and hold the leg, a very dangerous precedent (see figures 103, 104 and 106, 107).

It is worth noting that there are a few girls and an occasional boy who can throw the straight leg easily beyond 90° at the front if the leg and spine are held correctly, but cannot perform a *développé devant* above 90°, and this only after some year's training. As yet no valid reason has been found for this anomaly, although tight ham-strings being the cause have been eliminated. It seems certain that some children are born with a slight muscular deficiency in the region of pelvis, hip-joints and upper legs which does not show itself in normal life and not until after two or three years' work in classical dance. As it has not prevented several dancers of the Royal Ballet reaching stardom, no teacher should worry about this anomaly. They should nevertheless never allow any straining to gain height if the child shows an inability to straighten the knee fully in *développé devant* at 90° and above if there is any sign of pain or cramp as the leg is stretched outwards and refuses to go higher.

10. Dancers with Long Backs

Dancers with long backs will also have difficulty in producing an adequate *développé* in any direction because they will have tighter ligaments and muscles in the lumbar region to compensate for the added weight this places on the area. There are special exercises to increase mobility, but only to a certain degree. Such students are usually stiff and should be helped to loosen and strengthen the whole spine before attempting to raise or stretch the leg higher than 90°, or perform any elaborate *ports de bras* in which the bending of the body forwards plays a large part, a process which takes a long time.

It is this type of student who needs to use the full stretch of the working leg outwards when descending into *fondu*, lunging and when transferring weight from one leg to the other, always taking care that the spine is centred either directly above and just in front of the supporting instep when in *fondu*, or is directly centred midway between the two feet during the transfer. Dancers with long backs are also usually weak in the thoracic muscles. Time should be spent in trying to strengthen these by exercises for correct breathing and *cambrés* 1, 2– 5, 6, 7 (see pp. 56–66)

A careful centering of weight should also be observed with those whose upper leg is short in proportion to the whole because there is usually some tightness in the muscles from hip to knee as their length is impaired. The same exercises used to stretch tight ham-strings can also be of value if performed alternately with others useful in stretching the quadriceps, e.g. very slow *battements relevés* or *fondus* at 45°, in which the working leg is held momentarily at the height of the movement.

IV. ANOMALIES PREVENTING A FULL TURN-OUT

The function of the Y-shaped and pubo-femoral ligaments in the exercise of classical dance is not yet fully understood by most teachers and stems from the fact that not enough study has yet been made of how the relationship of a child's pelvis, and upper legs within the hip-joints change as the spine straightens and stretches with growth and the "baby tummy" disappears. It is known that at birth the angle of the baby's legs in their sockets may be said to be more "turned-out" than they are later when the legs have begun to straighten and strengthen, and the baby takes its first steps. The legs then become more firmly set in their sockets as the spine straightens and the child moves more steadily, its weight held firmly centred over the two legs. But no child should be taught to turn-out until at a far more advanced state of development.

An attempt has been made earlier to explain the function of the Y-shaped and pubo-femoral ligaments when turning-out (see p. 14). Yet no matter how carefully children are taught from time to time they suffer, particularly girls, from pain in the groins or a "clicking" at the hip-joints. When this occurs teachers should ask themselves whether too much stretching is taking place in this area, and have they taken into account the varying shapes of the pelvis, hip-joints and legs encountered in the dancing class? They should also ask themselves whether the muscles are all being used correctly and, above all, is the weight being correctly distributed.

It is already known that more women than men suffer from arthritic hip-joints and amongst these have been several dancers. Several answers have already been suggested for the reason. The most important would seem to be that too much importance was placed on turning-out the leg within the joint itself and centering its line, but not enough on stretching upwards from the pelvis and carrying the weight away from the legs. Whatever else the teacher may neglect, no child should ever be allowed "to sit on the hips".

Another reason suggested is that the girl did not have a good shape for dancing in the first place because the length of her spine from waist to coccyx was too long; or that the legs were naturally set too much to the front of the body and the turn-out then required was excessive, placing too much pressure on the joints themselves; or because the upper leg was too short and in her efforts to pull downwards from the hips to the knees and upwards from the hips to the waist, she neglected to keep the line of the legs fully centred by throwing the weight too far back on the lumbar region.

It is worth noting that if the Y-shaped and Pubo-femoral ligaments are shorter than normal this will not only hinder a leg rising past 90° at the front and side, but will also prevent even a well turned-out leg circling adequately in any form of *rond de jambe à terre* or *en l'air*. Something which occurs if the child is too long from hip to waist. Moreover not enough is yet known of the part played by the psoas in dance movements (see p. 53). It is unseen and cannot be felt. But it can be mentioned that if there is stiffness in the lower thoracic and lumbar regions and the child is unable to feel an absolutely straightened spine from the crown of the head to the coccyx, i.e. is unable to sit with the legs absolutely straight out in front with back against a wall, then there will be some difficulty in lifting the leg very high in any direction. Moreover if such children are forced to extend and lift the leg beyond their natural capacity, then groin trouble will undoubtedly ensue because they will "tuck the tail in" to gain a little more height.

With all children, particularly those having some difficulty with turn-out, it is always best to encourage them to use only as much turn-out as the strength and stretch of the muscles in the hip-joints and pelvic region of the spine allow.

V. PROBLEMS ARISING FROM INCORRECT USE OF THE KNEES

Man's knees take the weight of the body if there is anything wrong with his feet or toes. Therefore if he is standing incorrectly he compensates by taking the weight on his knees. Teachers may well ask why have several male dancers developed arthritic knees? The answer may be because they do not always place their weight correctly when dancing and particularly when lifting a partner. It is obvious in the latter case when they can frequently be seen to throw their weight too far backwards when lifting the girl from the floor, thus carrying her weight on chest and knees instead of through the spine and over the two feet or particular centre of balance, which in every case is determined by the need to combat the forces of gravity (see p. 92). Such failures to lift centrally through the legs and spine can also lead to serious back trouble as well as damaged knees.

This throwing the weight backwards has almost the same effect as "tucking in the tail" and must be avoided at all costs. It is particularly important with growing boys who frequently develop pains at the base of the patellas at that stage when their legs seem to be too long in proportion to their bodies and arms. It is now that the teacher must insist upon correct stance, weight well carried forwards and up through the spine to the crown of the head, as well as the stretch outwards of the arms from the shoulder sockets so that the latissimus dorsi, trapezius and recti abdominis are not allowed to slacken in their efforts to keep pace with the lengthening legs. It is also at this point of time when attention must be paid to the correct focus and level of the eyes. The boy must grow mentally as well as physically to his new height.

11. Sway-back Legs

Sway-back legs occur in both girls and boys and are usually due to poor physique and not a failure to stand correctly. The ligaments are long and the muscles at the back of the knee are over-stretched and need special exercises to help eliminate this problem as far as the natural growth and adjustment of the bones will allow.

Sway-back legs upset the distribution of the body weight and this can lead to several types of injury. Therefore those with an excessive degree should not be encouraged to venture into the field of classical dance. The joints most affected are the knees and the hips, and in some cases the ankles. There is too much pull on the back of the knee and not enough on the front, i.e. the student does not pull up his or her knees by the action of the quadriceps and muscles lying beneath because the biceps are longer than necessary to harmonise with the angle at which the trochanter is set in the hip socket, and the angle at which the femur is set in relationship to the lower leg at the knee joint. It is possible to re-educate the leg muscles to some degree with exercises designed to strengthen the quadriceps, which are usually weak. By carrying the weight well forwards and strengthening all the muscles in the pelvic and lumbar areas of the spine some students with sway-back legs can be taught to pull up the rectus femoris (i.e. the centre quadriceps muscles) and not pull the knee backwards (see p. 14). But the sway-back leg offers great difficulties.

VI. OCCUPATIONAL HAZARDS OF CLASSICAL DANCERS

The occupational hazard of classical dancers is the halus vulgus or bunion, which must not be confused with an enlarged toe joint, also caused by classical dance. It would appear that both occur through incorrect weight bearing and/or the wearing of too tight shoes.

It has been proved time and again, and is seen in photographs of the feet of well and little known dancers, that little or no damage will occur if the dancers themselves and their teachers pay the greatest attention to the centering of weight through the middle of the feet. Any deviation from the centre line to obtain the so-called "prettier" line is going to set up trouble because it thrusts the heel forwards i.e. "sickles" the foot outwards. This pushes the talus towards the big toe and thus the weight is not correctly distributed over as wide a field as possible. Moreover it prevents the dancer "feeling" the weight of the body descending and ascending directly through the centre bones of the leg (or legs) and spine.

The halus vulgus and enlarged toe joint can also begin to form if the muscles in front of the ankle are not allowed to relax and stretch accurately when descending and ascending in any form of *pliés* and *fondus*. Stress should always be made on the three points of balance of the foot when flat to the floor. i.e. Across the metatarsal arch from big to little toe joint and heel, and the need to keep the talus accurately balanced no matter to which height it is to be raised (see pp. 32–39).

12. Types of Arms

Just as there are various types of leg requiring extra care so there are different types of arm which may need more attention than others. These can be briefly summarised:

(a) The type of arm that does not move easily in its socket. This may be caused by short deltoid and trapezius muscles which can be stretched by insisting that all *ports de bras* be performed without any tension anywhere in the torso or head. If the joints are in any way stiff then some ease of movement can be acquired by encouraging the child to swing the arms to and fro, and round in their sockets whilst the shoulder-bones and blades are kept quite still. If the shoulders are narrow then care in breathing will help broaden the rib-cage and give more freedom to the muscles beneath the shoulder-blades to stretch outwards and thus broaden the movement of the arms.

(b) Children who may be said to have sway-back arms (!) do need more attention than most because they have to re-educate the muscles on the inside of the elbow to contract in order to hold the arm appropriately rounded. But they must do this without tensing those on the outside. These latter help to hold the rounded arm from beneath without straining the shoulders. But this will occur if the arm is lifted upwards and over from the back of the shoulders, and causes more tension and a distortion of the entire arm line so that its centre no longer runs through the bones from the armpit to the inside elbow and middle finger.

(c) Some boys and girls find it difficult to maintain a straight line through the centre of their arms to the middle finger, the hand dropping or "sickling" – so to speak – at the wrist. This is best cured by exercises to strengthen the muscles under the wrist because it will usually be found that such children have little strength on the outside of the arm and tend to drop their thumbs inwards. They need to be taught how to group and hold their fingers appropriately for their sex, instead, as in most cases, of being allowed to group them naturally when commencing *ports de bras* (see p. 55).

13. Short-sighted Children

Apart from the difficulty of only seeing objects near to them, short-sighted children are very handicapped when bending the head and spine backwards. Although it is valuable not to allow them to wear their spectacles and make them use what sight they have by placing them as near to the front of the class as convenient, then insisting upon the accuracy and placing of the lines and *épaulement*, the teacher must help them as much as possible when they practise any exercise entailing the curving of the head and spine backwards. In all such cases they should be told to turn and incline the head slightly to the left or right as soon as the head bend begins (see p. 63). This allows them to focus something at one or the other side, possibly another child's head and prevents them losing control. If the head is not so inclined as the cervical vertebrae increase their curve backwards, the eyes cease to focus anything at all, even a light on the ceiling. This is terrifying and causes the child either abruptly to bring the head upwards or allow it to fall backwards with a jerk. These movements can cause considerable pain either in the chest, or across the shoulders. If the instructions for *cambré 5* are carefully observed, a short-sighted child can benefit greatly from the controlled movement this allows the head and cervical vertebrae.

The short-sighted child will have initial difficulties when learning to turn, but provided he or she is taught to time the head movement correctly and use it accurately, after some practice he or she can usually turn as well and sometimes better than others with longer sight, because he or she frequently understands better the need for absolute control and accuracy of the focus of the eyes and head at the spot to which they must return.

14. Sinus Trouble, Common Colds etc.

There are perhaps no funnier even noisier sounds than a class of dancers suffering from colds in the head and performing *pirouettes*. The loud chorus of sniffs has to be heard to be believed. Everyone may laugh but any blockage of the sinuses of nose or ear should be taken seriously. The true centre of balance lies within the delicate membrane of the inner ear and is easily affected by excessive wax, catarrh, sinus-trouble and ear-ache. The teacher should watch carefully when colds are about that no child appears to lose undue control of balance or sense of direction. This is particularly so if the child is practising *pirouettes* because the inner ear is intimately connected with the true and swift focusing of the eyes, and is one of the chief reasons why every child must be taught how the eyes must focus a "spot" and swiftly return to that same spot if he or she is not to get giddy (see p. 90). This way of turning is quite unlike that of small children, who adore getting giddy, going round and round on one spot without focusing the eyes for the sheer joy of turning, falling down in a heap, then getting up somewhat dazedly to start again until laughter takes over and they lie relaxed on the floor laughing happily.

These instinctive attempts of tiny children to defy the forces of gravity contain the seeds of that love of sheer movement inspiring the efforts of all those who attempt to become classical dancers. It does not matter how tall or short, how fat

138 The straight line.

139 The body turns from the waist.

or thin, nor what physical difficulties they have to conquer, nor what problems are put in their way. As the great critic of music and ballet, Edwin Evans once said to my Father:—"If she really wants to dance as much as all that – then nothing will stop her".

His advice was taken. The road was long but worth all the happiness and joy in dance it has brought me as the following beautiful lines of one of the Royal Ballet students prove (figures 138, 139, 140).

140   The body curves.